The Great Minnesota Hot Dish

Your Cookbook for Classic Comfort Food

Revised & Updated

Theresa Millang
Karen Corbett

ADVENTURE PUBLICATIONS
Cambridge, Minnesota

DEDICATION

A special thank you to all who contributed to this cookbook, especially Karen Corbett for providing new recipes and Holly Harden for helping us make them modern.

Cover and book design by Lora Westberg

15 14 13 12 11 10 9 8

The Great Minnesota Hot Dish: Your Cookbook for Classic Comfort Food
First Edition 1999
Second Edition 2017
Copyright © 1999 and 2017 by Theresa Millang Estate and Karen Corbett
Published by Adventure Publications
An imprint of AdventureKEEN
310 Garfield Street South
Cambridge, Minnesota 55008
(800) 678-7006
www.adventurepublications.net
ISBN 978-1-59193-742-5 (pbk.); ISBN 978-1-59193-743-2 (ebook)

The Great Minnesota Hot Dish

Your Cookbook for Classic Comfort Food

Revised & Updated

TABLE OF CONTENTS

INTRODUCTION

We are pleased to present our updated second edition of this beloved classic, *The Great Minnesota Hot Dish*. Although we've added a few recipes and lots of "Make It Modern" tips, we have strived to retain the spirit of the charming original, first compiled by the late Theresa Millang. When Theresa first moved to Minnesota, she found three things especially interesting about the state. First, Minnesota weather is not only beautiful in the summer, but it's also great for skiing in the winter. Second, "Minnesota Nice" is a quality to admire. And, third, the Minnesota Hot Dish is something most other folks would call a "casserole." This cookbook is an ode to the Minnesota Hot Dish.

A hot dish is a combination of one or more ingredients, usually including meat, fish, or fowl; noodles, rice, or grains; and a sauce and vegetables to give it texture and color. All of the ingredients are put together into one baking dish (be it glass, porcelain, iron, ceramic, etc.) and placed in the oven, to be brought out as one complete meal.

In Minnesota, there are hot dishes for different occasions. There's the "company" hot dish, which has a more elegant presentation and may include seafood but not tuna. The "baby shower" hot dish may indeed contain tuna. Then there's the hot dish you serve at funerals, the contents of which depend upon your area. The "neighbor is sick" hot dish may contain ground beef and macaroni in tomato sauce. There's the "potluck" hot dish, which could be a bean or corn side-dish hot dish. There's the "brunch" hot dish with eggs, of course, or perhaps a bubbly fruit cobbler dessert hot dish. You are expected to serve bread and maybe a salad alongside a hot dish.

This cookbook features recipes dating back to the early 1900s, a time when many cooks did not include specific amounts, cooking times, or oven temperatures in their recordings; a sampling of these are from Theresa's Scandinavian mother-in-law's recipe collection. Other recipes are from the

1950s, when canned soup came full force into the market, a boon to the homemaker. This eased the preparation of many a hot dish, with canned tuna becoming a favorite ingredient. As the years marched on, Minnesota, heavily populated with those of Scandinavian heritage, began to incorporate international flavors into new hot dishes. Tex-Mex became very popular. Then came Cajun, Creole, Southern, and Chinese-style hot dishes. The possibilities are endless.

Today's hot dishes use a lot of the same ingredients but in different combinations. There are lots of fresh, new ingredients on the market, and many convenient canned sauces and seasoning packets help in preparing quick, delicious meals. One great advantage of hot dishes is that you can prepare most of them in advance, and then refrigerate or freeze them until you're ready to bake.

The hot dish recipes in this cookbook are organized in the following chapters: Poultry, Beef, Pork, Seafood, and Eggs. There's a hot dish here for every occasion, and our wish is that you will enjoy this collection with your friends and family, whether you're in Minnesota or anywhere in the world.

Poultry

Baked Beans, Rice, and Chicken

INGREDIENTS

- 2 **tablespoons corn oil**
- 6 **boneless, skinless chicken breast halves, cut into strips and seasoned with salt and black pepper**
- 1 **cup long-grain white rice, uncooked**
- ½ **cup chopped onion**
- ½ **cup chopped green bell pepper**
- 2 **cloves garlic, chopped**
- 1 **teaspoon chili powder**
- 2 **cups chicken broth or water**
- 1 **(14.5-ounce) can stewed tomatoes**
- 1 **(16-ounce) can baked beans**

Preheat oven to 375˚F.

Heat oil in a saucepan over medium heat. Add chicken; stir and cook until browned. Transfer chicken to a large bowl, reserving oil in pan. Add rice, onion, bell pepper, and garlic to saucepan; cook while stirring 2 minutes. Stir rice mixture into bowl with chicken. Add chili powder, chicken broth, tomatoes, and beans; mix well. Spoon mixture into a lightly greased 13x9x2-inch glass baking dish. Cover with aluminum foil. Bake 50 minutes or until rice is cooked. Serves 6.

Note: Serve this hot dish with a tossed salad and warm crusty bread.

Chicken, Rice, and Beans Hot Dish

INGREDIENTS

- 1 cup long-grain white rice, uncooked
- ½ cup chicken broth
- ½ cup chopped onion, cooked in butter 5 minutes
- 1 (16-ounce) can hot chili beans in sauce, undrained
- 1 (16-ounce) can pinto beans, drained
- 1 (10-ounce) package frozen chopped broccoli, thawed
- 8 slices bacon
- 4 boneless, skinless chicken breast halves, lightly seasoned with salt and ground black pepper
- 1 cup shredded Monterey Jack cheese with jalapeño peppers

Preheat oven to 350°F.

Mix together rice, chicken broth, onion, beans, and broccoli in a large bowl. Pour rice mixture into a lightly greased, shallow, 2-quart glass baking dish. Wrap 2 slices of bacon around each chicken breast half. Place chicken on top of rice mixture. Bake, uncovered, 55 minutes or until chicken is no longer pink. Remove from oven. Sprinkle with cheese, and bake until cheese is melted. Serves 4.

Note: Serve this hot dish with a crisp green salad.

Biscuit-Topped Chicken Hot Dish

INGREDIENTS

- 2 **cups cubed cooked chicken**
- 2 **(10½-ounce) cans condensed cream of chicken soup, undiluted**
- 1 **(16-ounce) package frozen mixed vegetables, thawed**
- 1 **teaspoon grated onion**
- ½ **cup whole milk**
- 1 **egg, lightly beaten**
- 1 **cup boxed biscuit mix**

Preheat oven to 400°F.

Combine chicken, soup, vegetables, and onion in a lightly greased 2½-quart oval glass baking dish; spread evenly. Stir together milk, egg, and biscuit mix in a bowl. Pour milk mixture over chicken mixture. Bake, uncovered, 35 minutes or until bubbly and biscuits are golden. Serves 6.

Note: This hot dish is like a homemade pot pie. A salad will complete the meal.

Chicken-and-Biscuit Hot Dish

INGREDIENTS

- 4 cups chicken, cooked and diced
- 1 (10½-ounce) can condensed cream of chicken soup, undiluted
- 1 (10½-ounce) can condensed cream of mushroom soup, undiluted
- 1 cup frozen peas, thawed
- 1½ cups shredded Cheddar cheese, divided
- 1½ cups flour
- 2 teaspoons baking powder
- ½ tsp salt
- ¼ cup margarine
- ½ cup milk

Preheat oven to 400°F.

Cook chicken, soups, peas, and 1 cup cheese in a large saucepan over medium heat until hot and bubbly. Pour chicken mixture into an ungreased 9x13-inch baking pan. Combine flour, baking powder, and salt in a bowl. Cut butter into flour mixture with a pastry cutter or fork. Add milk, and stir with a fork until mixture forms a soft dough. Turn dough out onto a lightly floured surface. Knead gently until no longer sticky. Roll to ½-inch thickness. Cut into biscuits using a 2-inch-round floured cutter. Arrange biscuits over hot chicken mixture. Bake 18–22 minutes or until biscuits are golden. Sprinkle with remaining ½ cup cheese. Bake 5 minutes. Serves 6.

Baked Macaroni and Cheese with Chicken

INGREDIENTS

- 8 ounces elbow macaroni
- 2 tablespoons butter
- 2 cloves garlic, minced
- 1 (14.5-ounce) can diced tomatoes
- 1 pound Velveeta
- ½ cup sour cream
- ⅔ cup half-and-half
- 1 teaspoon ground cumin
- 1 teaspoon cayenne pepper
- 2–4 cups shredded rotisserie chicken
- 2 cups Cheddar cheese

Preheat oven to 400˚F.

Cook macaroni; drain. Melt butter in a large skillet over medium heat. Stir in garlic, and cook 1 minute. Add diced tomatoes, and cook until liquid is evaporated. Shred Velveeta; stir into tomato mixture until cheese is melted. Stir in sour cream, half-and-half, cumin, pepper, chicken, and macaroni. Pour mixture into a lightly greased 13x9x2-inch baking dish. Sprinkle with Cheddar cheese. Bake 10 minutes. Serves 6.

 Make It Modern: Substitute 2 diced fresh tomatoes for canned tomatoes.

Chicken-Broccoli-Rotini Hot Dish

INGREDIENTS

- 1 **tablespoon corn oil**
- 4 **boneless, skinless chicken breasts, cut into chunks**
- 1 **small onion, minced**
- 1 **(14.5-ounce) can chicken broth**
- 3 **cups rotini pasta, cooked 5 minutes according to package directions and drained**
- 8 **ounces Velveeta, cubed**
- 1 **(10-ounce) package frozen chopped broccoli, thawed**

Preheat oven to 350°F.

Heat oil in a large saucepan over medium heat. Add chicken and onion; stir and cook until chicken is no longer pink. Stir in broth. Bring to a boil. Stir in rotini, cheese, and broccoli; mix well. Pour mixture into a lightly greased 2-quart baking dish. Cover and bake 25 minutes or until rotini is tender. Serves 6.

Note: Serve with a lettuce-and-tomato salad.

Chicken Linguine Hot Dish

INGREDIENTS

- 2 cups cubed cooked chicken
- 1 (9-ounce) package refrigerated linguine, rinsed with hot water and drained
- 1 (10½-ounce) can condensed cream of chicken soup, undiluted and heated
- 1 cup chicken broth, heated
- ½ cup finely chopped onion
- 1 tablespoon chopped fresh parsley
- ½ cup diced green bell pepper
- Pinch ground black pepper
- 3 plum tomatoes, cut into wedges
- 3 tablespoons sliced green onion
- ½ cup shredded Cheddar cheese

Preheat oven to 350°F.

Combine chicken and next 7 ingredients in a large bowl. Spoon chicken mixture into a lightly greased 8x8x2-inch glass baking dish. Bake, uncovered, 40 minutes or until thoroughly heated and bubbly. Top with tomatoes, green onion, and cheese. Bake, uncovered, until cheese is melted. Serves 6.

Note: Serve with salad and warm, crusty bread.

Chicken Noodle Hot Dish

INGREDIENTS

- 3¾ cups wide egg noodles, uncooked
- 1 (10½-ounce) can condensed cream of chicken soup, undiluted
- 1¾ cups milk
- 2 cups chopped cooked chicken
- 1 (10-ounce) package frozen chopped broccoli, thawed
- 1 tablespoon minced yellow onion
- ¼ teaspoon garlic powder
- 6 tablespoons grated Parmesan cheese
- ¼ teaspoon ground black pepper

Preheat oven to 350°F.

Cook noodles 3 fewer minutes than listed on package directions; drain. Stir together soup and milk in a large saucepan over medium heat until hot. Add chicken and next 5 ingredients, and stir until blended; stir in noodles. Spoon mixture into a lightly greased 2-quart baking dish. Cover and bake 30 minutes or until hot and bubbly. Sprinkle with additional Parmesan cheese, if desired. Serves 4.

Note: Serve this hot dish with salad and buttered bread.

Make It Modern: Use 1 bunch fresh broccoli, chopped and blanched, instead of frozen broccoli.

Chicken-Pasta Barbecue Bake

INGREDIENTS

- 1 **pound rotini pasta**
- 1 **can whole kernel corn, undrained**
- 1½ **cups barbecue sauce**
- ⅓ **cup half-and-half**
- ½ **teaspoon salt**
- ¼ **teaspoon pepper**
- 2 **cups rotisserie chicken, shredded**
- 2 **cups shredded mozzarella cheese**

Preheat oven to 350°F.

Cook pasta according to package directions; drain. Combine corn, barbecue sauce, half-and-half, salt, and pepper in a saucepan over medium heat. Stir in pasta and shredded chicken. Pour into a lightly greased 9x13-inch pan. Sprinkle cheese evenly over top. Bake 15 minutes, and serve hot. Serves 6.

Jeanne's Chicken-Mac

INGREDIENTS

3½ cups elbow macaroni, uncooked

2 cups cubed cooked chicken

1 cup shredded Cheddar cheese

1 (2-ounce) jar diced pimientos or
   2 tablespoons chopped roasted
   sweet red bell peppers plus
   2 tablespoons water

3 tablespoons minced onion

2 cloves garlic, minced

½ teaspoon salt

Pinch black pepper

½ teaspoon curry powder

1 (10½-ounce) can condensed
   cream of chicken soup, undiluted

1 cup whole milk

1 (4-ounce) can mushroom stems
   and pieces, undrained

Preheat oven to 350°F.

Place all ingredients into a lightly greased 2-quart glass baking dish; mix well. Cover and bake 1 hour. Serves 4.

Note: Jeanne is a home economist. Many years ago, she told me about using uncooked pasta in certain hot dishes, and this is one of them. Serve this easy-to-prepare hot dish with a crisp green salad.

Cheesy Chicken and Pasta

INGREDIENTS

- 2 tablespoons butter
- ¼ cup chopped onion
- 2 tablespoons all-purpose flour
- 1¼ cups whole milk
- 2 (8-ounce) packages frozen creamy Cheddar vegetables and pasta
- 1½ cups cubed cooked chicken
- ¼ cup dry breadcrumbs, mixed with 1 tablespoon melted butter

Preheat oven to 350°F.

Melt butter in a large saucepan over medium heat. Add onion; stir and cook until tender. Gradually stir in flour. Gradually add milk, stirring constantly, until thickened. Stir in frozen vegetable-pasta mixture and chicken. Pour chicken mixture into a lightly greased 1½-quart glass baking dish. Sprinkle breadcrumb mixture on top. Bake 35 to 45 minutes or until thoroughly heated. Serves 4.

Note: Serve with sliced tomatoes and rolls.

Anne's Chicken and Rice

INGREDIENTS

- 1 (6-ounce) package long-grain and wild rice mix, uncooked
- 2 tablespoons corn oil
- 6 meaty, skinless chicken thighs, lightly seasoned with salt and ground black pepper
- ½ cup chopped onion
- ½ cup sliced celery
- 1 (4.5-ounce) jar whole mushrooms, drained
- 1 (10½-ounce) can condensed cream of chicken soup, mixed with 2 cups cold water

Preheat oven to 350°F.

Spread rice into a lightly greased 13x9x2-inch baking dish. Sprinkle evenly with seasoning mix from packet. Heat oil in a saucepan over medium heat. Add chicken; brown slightly. Remove chicken; place over rice. Add onion to saucepan; stir and cook 2 minutes. Spoon onion over chicken. Place sliced celery and mushrooms around chicken. Add soup mixture to saucepan, and bring to a boil; pour over all ingredients in baking dish. Cover and bake 1 hour. Uncover and bake 20 minutes or until chicken is done. Serves 6.

Note: Serve this meaty hot dish with a shredded cabbage-and-carrot salad tossed with Italian dressing.

 Make It Modern: Substitute 4–5 ounces sliced baby bella mushrooms sautéed in butter for jarred mushrooms.

Chicken Hot Dish

INGREDIENTS

- 5 tablespoons butter
- 6 tablespoons all-purpose flour
- 1¾ cups whole milk
- 1 cup chicken broth
- 2½ cups cubed cooked chicken
- 1¾ cups cooked long-grain white rice
- ½ teaspoon salt
- Pinch black pepper
- ⅓ cup chopped green bell pepper
- 2 tablespoons minced onion
- 1 (4-ounce) can mushroom stems and pieces, drained
- ⅓ cup slivered almonds

Preheat oven to 350°F.

Melt butter in a large saucepan over medium heat. Gradually stir in flour; cook while stirring 1 minute. Add milk and chicken broth. Bring to a boil, stirring constantly; stir and cook 1 minute. Add chicken and next 7 ingredients; mix well. Spoon mixture into a lightly greased 2½-quart glass baking dish. Bake, uncovered, 45–50 minutes or until very hot and bubbly. Serves 6.

Note: Serve with buttered peas and soft buttered rolls.

Chicken-Peas Hot Dish

INGREDIENTS

- 2 tablespoons corn oil
- 4 boneless, skinless chicken breast halves, seasoned with salt and ground black pepper
- 1 cup chopped onion
- 1 cup long-grain white rice, uncooked
- 1 medium-size red bell pepper, coarsely chopped
- ¼ teaspoon salt
- ¼ teaspoon ground turmeric
- ¼ teaspoon crushed red pepper flakes
- 2 cups chicken broth
- ½ cup frozen sweet peas, thawed

Preheat oven to 350°F.

Heat corn oil in a saucepan over medium-high heat. Add chicken; quickly brown on both sides. Remove chicken and keep warm. Add chopped onion to saucepan; stir and cook until tender but not brown. Add rice, bell pepper, and next 3 ingredients; stir and cook 1 minute. Stir in chicken broth; bring to a boil. Spoon rice mixture into a lightly greased 3-quart baking dish. Place chicken on top of rice mixture; press down lightly. Cover and bake 35 minutes; stir in peas, and cook 10 more minutes or until rice is tender and chicken is no longer pink. Fluff rice just before serving. Serves 4.

Note: Serve with a green salad tossed with Italian dressing.

Chicken Rice-A-Roni Hot Dish

INGREDIENTS

- 1 (6.9-ounce) package Rice-A-Roni
- 1 (10-ounce) package frozen broccoli
- 2 cups diced cooked chicken
- 1 cup Cheddar cheese, grated
- 1 cup milk
- ½ cup margarine
- 1 (10½-ounce) can cream of chicken soup, undiluted

Preheat oven to 350°F.

Prepare Rice-A-Roni according to package directions. Cook broccoli according to package directions. Layer rice, broccoli, chicken, and cheese in a lightly greased 9x13-inch pan. Heat milk, margarine, and cream of chicken soup in a saucepan over medium heat, stirring until combined. Pour milk mixture over cheese. Top with additional cheese, if desired. Bake 45 minutes. Serves 6.

Chicken-Rice-Nut Hot Dish

INGREDIENTS

- 2 **tablespoons corn oil**
- 4 **boneless, skinless chicken breast halves, lightly seasoned with salt and ground black pepper**
- 1 **cup chopped onion**
- 3 **large cloves garlic, chopped**
- 1 **(6-ounce) package seasoned quick-cooking long-grain and wild rice mix**
- 2 **cups water, boiling hot**
- 1 **(2-ounce) jar diced pimientos, drained (optional)**
- 6 **tablespoons coarsely chopped walnuts**

Chopped fresh parsley

Preheat oven to 350°F.

Heat oil in a saucepan over medium-high heat. Add chicken, onion, and garlic. Brown chicken well on all sides; remove chicken from pan. Add rice; cook while stirring 1 minute. Stir in water and seasoning packet. Stir in pimientos, if desired, and nuts. Spoon rice mixture into a lightly greased, shallow, 8-inch-square baking dish. Place chicken on top of rice mixture; press down slightly into rice. Cover and bake 45 minutes or until rice is tender and chicken is no longer pink. Garnish with parsley. Serves 4.

Note: Serve with a crisp salad, steamed broccoli, and your favorite bread or rolls.

Chicken Veggies 'n' Rice

INGREDIENTS

- 2 tablespoons butter
- 2 tablespoons corn oil
- 6 boneless chicken thighs, lightly seasoned with salt and pepper
- 1 cup long-grain white rice, uncooked
- 2 cloves garlic, chopped
- 1½ cups tomato-vegetable juice
- 1 cup water
- 1 (4-ounce) can mushroom stems and pieces, drained
- 1 cup chopped onion
- 1 cup chopped celery
- ¼ cup sliced black olives
- 1 teaspoon salt
- ¼ teaspoon black pepper
- ½ teaspoon dried marjoram, crushed
- Pinch crushed saffron
- 1 cup frozen peas, thawed
- 1 cup fresh tomato wedges, lightly salted

Preheat oven to 375°F.

Melt butter in oil in a saucepan over medium heat; cook chicken in butter mixture until browned on both sides. Remove chicken; keep warm. Add rice to saucepan; stir and cook until golden. Add garlic; stir and cook 1 minute. Stir in vegetable juice and water. Stir in mushrooms and next 7 ingredients. Spoon rice mixture into a lightly greased 13x9x2-inch glass baking dish. Top with chicken, pressing lightly into mixture. Cover with aluminum foil. Bake 1 hour. Remove from oven. Sprinkle peas evenly over dish. Top with tomato wedges. Cover; return to oven. Bake 20 minutes. Serves 6.

Note: Serve this delicious hot dish with a crisp lettuce, broccoli, and cauliflower salad tossed with Italian dressing and some hard rolls.

Chicken with Wild Rice

INGREDIENTS

- ¾ cup long-grain and wild rice, uncooked
- 2 tablespoons butter
- 1 medium-size onion, chopped
- 2 cloves garlic, finely chopped
- ½ cup chopped green bell pepper
- ¼ cup chopped celery
- 3 tablespoons chopped parsley
- 3 tablespoons chopped pimientos
- 2 (4-ounce) cans sliced mushrooms, drained
- 2½ cups diced cooked chicken
- 3 cups chicken broth
- ½ cup sour cream
- ½ cup sliced water chestnuts
- ½ cup slivered almonds
- ¼ teaspoon dried sage
- ¼ teaspoon dried thyme, crumbled
- Pinch ground black pepper

Preheat oven to 350°F.

Cook rice according to package directions; keep warm. Melt butter in a saucepan over medium heat. Add onion, garlic, and green pepper; cook while stirring until soft. Add celery to pan; cook while stirring 1 minute. Transfer onion mixture to a large bowl; stir in parsley and next 10 ingredients until well blended. Gradually stir in rice. Spoon mixture into a lightly buttered 2½-quart glass baking dish. Cover and bake 50 minutes. Serves 6.

Note: Serve this hot dish with green salad, steamed broccoli, and jellied cranberry sauce.

Kathleen's Chicken Hot Dish

INGREDIENTS

- 5 tablespoons butter
- 6 tablespoons all-purpose flour
- 1¾ cups whole milk
- 1 cup chicken broth
- 2½ cups cubed cooked chicken
- 1¾ cups cooked long-grain white rice
- ½ teaspoon salt
- Pinch ground black pepper
- ⅓ cup chopped green bell pepper
- 2 tablespoons minced onion
- 1 (4-ounce) can mushroom stems and pieces, drained
- ½ cup slivered almonds

Preheat oven to 350°F.

Melt butter in a large saucepan over medium heat. Gradually stir in flour; cook while stirring 1 minute. Add milk and chicken broth. Bring to a boil, stirring constantly; cook 1 minute. Add chicken and next 7 ingredients; mix well. Spoon chicken mixture into a lightly greased 2½-quart glass baking dish. Bake, uncovered, 45–50 minutes or until very hot and bubbly. Serves 6.

Note: This hot dish is ready for the oven in minutes. Serve with buttered peas and soft rolls (also buttered, of course).

Lottie's Chicken Hot Dish

INGREDIENTS

- 2 cups cubed cooked chicken
- ½ cup chopped onion
- 2 stalks celery, diced
- 1 tablespoon diced pimientos
- 1 tablespoon fresh lemon juice
- 1 teaspoon prepared mustard
- ¼ teaspoon salt
- ¼ teaspoon black pepper
- ½ cup mayonnaise
- 3 hard-boiled eggs, chopped
- ½ cup slivered almonds
- 2 cups cooked long-grain white rice
- 1 (10½-ounce) can condensed cream of chicken soup, undiluted
- 1½ cups crushed potato chips

Preheat oven to 375°F.

Combine first 13 ingredients in a large bowl. Spoon mixture into a lightly greased 13x9x2-inch glass baking dish. Sprinkle with potato chips. Bake, uncovered, 35 minutes or until very hot. Serves 6.

Note: Serve with buttered green beans, a fresh fruit salad, and your favorite warm rolls.

 Make It Modern: Substitute 1½ cups Panko breadcrumbs for crushed potato chips.

Manie's Chicken-Rice Hot Dish

INGREDIENTS

- 1 **cup long-grain and wild rice, uncooked**
- ½ **teaspoon salt**
- 3 **cups water**
- 1 **tablespoon butter**
- 1 **cup chopped onion**
- 1 **cup thinly sliced celery**
- 1 **cup shredded fresh carrots**
- 1 **(14.5-ounce) can chicken broth**
- 2 **cups half-and-half**
- ¼ **cup all-purpose flour**
- 2 **tablespoons cooking sherry or apple juice**
- ¾ **teaspoon salt**
- ¼ **teaspoon ground black pepper**
- 3 **cups cubed cooked chicken**
- 5 **tablespoons dried cranberries**
- 5 **tablespoons sliced natural almonds, toasted**

Preheat oven to 350˚F.

Bring rice, salt, and 3 cups water to a boil in a medium saucepan. Reduce heat; cover and simmer 50 minutes, and drain in a colander. Melt butter in a saucepan over medium heat. Add onion, celery, and carrots; cook while stirring 10 minutes. Add broth; bring to a boil. Whisk together half-and-half and flour in a bowl until smooth; gradually whisk into boiling broth. Stir in sherry, salt, and pepper. Bring to a boil. Reduce heat; simmer 5 minutes. Pour broth mixture into a large bowl. Add chicken and rice; mix well. Spoon into a lightly greased, shallow 2½-quart baking dish. Cover and bake 40 minutes, stirring once. Remove from oven. Sprinkle with cranberries and almonds. Let stand 10 minutes before serving. Serves 8.

Note: With wild rice, sweet cranberries, and toasted almonds, guests will purr over this hot dish!

Mr. Brown's Chicken and Rice

INGREDIENTS

2 tablespoons corn oil

1 cup chopped onion

½ medium-size green bell pepper, chopped

2 cloves garlic, coarsely chopped

¾ cup chopped celery

¼ cup chopped parsley

6 boneless, skinless chicken breast halves, cut into strips

½ teaspoon salt

¼ teaspoon black pepper

1 cup long-grain white rice, uncooked

1 (14.5-ounce) can stewed tomatoes, drained and cut up

1½ cups tomato-vegetable juice

1 (4-ounce) can mushroom stems and pieces, drained

1 cup chicken broth

Preheat oven to 375°F.

Heat oil in a saucepan over medium heat. Add onion, green pepper, garlic, celery, and parsley. Cook while stirring 1 minute; remove onion mixture to a large bowl, reserving oil in pan. Season chicken with salt and pepper; add to saucepan, and cook until lightly browned. Remove chicken to bowl with onion mixture. Add rice to saucepan; stir and cook 2 minutes. Remove rice to bowl with onion mixture and chicken; stir in tomatoes and next 3 ingredients. Spoon into a lightly greased 11½x7½x1¾-inch glass baking dish. Cover tightly with aluminum foil. Bake 1 hour. Uncover and bake 10 minutes. Serves 6.

Note: Mr. Brown will sometimes toss a half-dozen cleaned raw shrimp into this hot dish along with the chicken. Serve this hot dish with a mixture of salad greens tossed with Italian dressing.

One-Dish Chicken 'n' Rice

INGREDIENTS

- **1 (10½-ounce) can condensed cream of mushroom soup, undiluted**
- **¾ cup whole milk**
- **½ cup water**
- **½ cup long-grain white rice, uncooked**
- **1 (4.5-ounce) jar whole button mushrooms, drained (optional)**
- **¼ teaspoon paprika**
- **4 boneless, skinless chicken breast halves, lightly seasoned with salt and ground black pepper**

Preheat oven to 350°F.

Mix together first 6 ingredients in a lightly greased, shallow 2-quart glass baking dish. Place chicken on top of rice mixture. Cover and bake 45 minutes or until chicken and rice are done. Serves 4.

Note: This recipe can easily be changed by adding frozen or blanched fresh broccoli cuts, grated onion, etc. Theresa first saw the recipe on a soup can, and it's very easy to prepare.

Cashew Chicken Hot Dish

INGREDIENTS

- 2 tablespoons butter
- 4 boneless, skinless chicken breast halves, cut into cubes
- 1 medium-size onion, diced
- 2 (4-ounce) cans sliced mushrooms, drained
- 1 cup long-grain white rice, uncooked
- 1 tablespoon chicken bouillon granules, mixed with 1½ cups boiling water
- 1 teaspoon ground ginger
- 2 cups frozen or blanched fresh broccoli pieces
- 1 cup cashew nuts, divided

Pinch ground black pepper

- 1 teaspoon soy sauce (optional)

Garnish: Parsley sprigs

Preheat oven to 375°F.

Melt butter in a saucepan over medium heat; add chicken, and cook 5 minutes or until done. Spoon chicken into a lightly greased 2½-quart round glass baking dish. Add onion, mushrooms, rice, bouillon mixture, and ginger; mix well. Cover and bake 30 minutes. Stir in broccoli; bake 10 minutes or until vegetables are done. Remove from oven; let stand 5 minutes. Stir in ½ cup cashews, pepper, and, if desired, soy sauce. Sprinkle remaining ½ cup cashews on top. Place under broiler (uncovered) to brown. Remove from oven. Garnish, if desired. Serves 4.

Note: Serve with fresh matchstick carrots, an orange-pineapple molded gelatin salad, and crusty rolls.

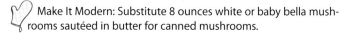 Make It Modern: Substitute 8 ounces white or baby bella mushrooms sautéed in butter for canned mushrooms.

Chicken Chow Mein

INGREDIENTS

- ¼ cup butter
- ½ cup chopped onion
- 2 stalks celery, chopped
- 1 (10½-ounce) can condensed cream of mushroom soup, undiluted
- ½ cup chicken broth
- 1 tablespoon soy sauce
- 3 cups cubed cooked chicken
- ½ cup sliced fresh mushrooms
- 1½ cups chow mein noodles
- 5 tablespoons salted cashew halves

Preheat oven to 350°F.

Melt butter in a large saucepan over medium heat. Add onion and celery, and cook until tender. Stir in soup, chicken broth, and soy sauce. Add chicken and mushrooms; stir and cook until hot. Pour chicken mixture into a lightly greased 2-quart baking dish. Sprinkle with chow mein noodles and cashews. Bake, uncovered, 25 minutes or until bubbly and hot. Serves 4.

Note: For extra color and flavor, add 1 tablespoon chopped red bell pepper before baking.

 Make It Modern: Try making your own cream of mushroom soup (see page 229).

Cheddar Chicken and Asparagus

INGREDIENTS

- 1½ **pounds fresh asparagus spears, halved, partially cooked, and drained**
- 2 **tablespoons corn oil**
- 4 **boneless, skinless chicken breast halves**
- ½ **teaspoon salt**
- ¼ **teaspoon black pepper**
- 1 **(10½-ounce) can condensed cream of chicken soup, undiluted**
- ½ **cup mayonnaise**
- 1 **teaspoon lemon juice**
- ½ **teaspoon curry powder**
- 1 **cup shredded Cheddar cheese**

Preheat oven to 375°F.

Place asparagus into a lightly greased 9x9-inch square glass baking dish. Heat oil in a saucepan over medium heat. Season chicken with salt and pepper; cook chicken in oil in saucepan until brown on both sides. Place chicken over asparagus. Combine soup, mayonnaise, lemon juice, and curry powder in a bowl; mix well, and pour over chicken. Cover and bake 40 to 50 minutes or until chicken is tender and juices run clear. Sprinkle with Cheddar cheese. Remove from oven. Let stand 5 minutes before serving. Serves 4.

Note: This makes a good luncheon hot dish when served with an assortment of breads and fresh fruit.

 Make It Modern: Substitute ½ cup plain yogurt or cottage cheese for mayonnaise.

Curried Chicken Hot Dish

INGREDIENTS

- 4 cups cooked long-grain white rice
- 2 cups cubed cooked chicken or turkey
- ½ cup cubed cooked smoked sausage or ham
- 1 (8-ounce) can water chestnuts, drained and coarsely chopped
- 1 (10½-ounce) can condensed cream of chicken soup, undiluted
- 1½ cups whole milk
- ½ cup mayonnaise (not salad dressing)
- ¼ cup minced fresh parsley
- 2 tablespoons minced yellow onion
- ¾ teaspoon salt
- ¼ teaspoon curry powder
- 6 tablespoons sliced almonds

Preheat oven to 350°F.

Spoon rice into a lightly greased 13x9x2-inch baking dish. Top evenly with chicken, sausage, and water chestnuts. Combine soup and next 6 ingredients in a bowl; mix well, and pour over chicken mixture. Cover and bake 35 minutes or until hot and bubbly. Remove cover; sprinkle with sliced almonds. Bake 5 minutes. Serves 6.

Note: Serve with a mixed greens salad and hard rolls.

Chicken Cordon Bleu

INGREDIENTS

- 4 boneless, skinless chicken breast halves, flattened to ¼-inch thickness
- 2 teaspoons Dijon mustard
- ½ cup shredded Swiss cheese
- ½ cup fully cooked ham, chopped
- 2 tablespoons minced pimientos
- 1 tablespoon minced green bell pepper
- 1 egg, lightly beaten
- 2 tablespoons cold water
- 5 tablespoons all-purpose flour, mixed with ¼ teaspoon salt
- 6 tablespoons dry breadcrumbs
- Corn oil

Preheat oven to 350°F.

Spread chicken breasts with mustard. Mix together cheese, ham, pimientos, and green bell pepper in a bowl; place equal portions cheese mixture in center of each chicken breast. Bring one end of breast over cheese mixture. Fold in sides; roll up, jellyroll fashion, pressing ends to seal. Mix together egg and water in a bowl. Place flour mixture and breadcrumbs in two separate bowls. Dip each chicken breast roll in egg mixture, then coat with flour; dip back into egg mixture, then roll in breadcrumbs. Refrigerate 1 hour. Pour oil to depth of 1 inch in a large frying pan. Fry each chicken breast roll until browned. Place chicken breast rolls in a lightly greased 8-inch square baking dish. Bake 30 minutes or until chicken is no longer pink. Serves 4.

Note: Serve this "blue ribbon" dish with rice pilaf and buttered steamed asparagus spears.

Easy Chicken Divan

INGREDIENTS

- 2 (10-ounce) packages frozen chopped broccoli, cooked according to package directions
- 2 cups diced cooked chicken
- 2 (10½-ounce) cans condensed cream of chicken soup, undiluted
- ½ cup mayonnaise
- ½ cup shredded Cheddar cheese
- 1½ cups croutons

Preheat oven to 350°F.

Place broccoli in a lightly greased 13x9x2-inch baking dish. Cover with chicken. Blend together soup and mayonnaise in a small bowl, and spread soup mixture over chicken. Sprinkle evenly with cheese and croutons. Bake 30 minutes. Serves 6.

Make It Modern: Substitute ½ cup plain yogurt or cottage cheese for mayonnaise and 1 bunch trimmed fresh broccoli (lightly steamed) for frozen broccoli.

Sam's Chicken Divan

INGREDIENTS

- 1 (16-ounce) package frozen broccoli cuts, cooked according to package directions and drained
- 2 cups cubed cooked boneless, skinless chicken breast halves
- 1 tablespoon toasted slivered almonds
- 1 (10½-ounce) can condensed cream of chicken soup, undiluted
- ½ cup mayonnaise
- 1 teaspoon fresh lemon juice
- ½ cup shredded Cheddar cheese
- 6 tablespoons dry breadcrumbs, mixed with 2 tablespoons melted butter

Preheat oven to 350°F.

Place broccoli in a lightly greased 12x8-inch glass baking dish. Layer chicken over broccoli. Sprinkle with almonds. Mix together soup, mayonnaise, and lemon juice in a bowl; spoon soup mixture over almonds. Sprinkle with cheese. Top with breadcrumb mixture. Bake, uncovered, 35 minutes or until very hot. Serves 4.

Note: This is a good company dish. Serve with a nice salad and rolls. Sam often adds cooked rice on the bottom, then proceeds with the recipe as directed.

Chicken Cacciatore

INGREDIENTS

- 1¼ cups quick-cooking rice, uncooked
- 2 tablespoons chopped fresh parsley, divided
- 1 (14.5-ounce) can chicken broth
- 1 (6-ounce) can tomato paste
- 1 (4-ounce) can sliced mushrooms, drained
- ¾ cup water
- ¼ cup dry white wine or apple juice
- 1 medium-size onion, chopped
- ¼ cup chopped green bell pepper
- 1¼ teaspoons dried basil
- 1 teaspoon garlic salt
- ½ teaspoon Italian seasoning
- ¼ teaspoon black pepper
- 6 boneless, skinless chicken breast halves
- 1 cup shredded mozzarella cheese
- ¼ cup grated Parmesan cheese

Preheat oven to 350°F.

Spread rice in bottom of a lightly greased 13x9x2-inch glass baking dish. Combine 1 tablespoon parsley and next 11 ingredients in a large bowl. Pour parsley mixture over rice. Arrange chicken on top of rice. Cover and bake 50 minutes. Uncover; sprinkle with mozzarella and Parmesan cheeses. Bake 5 minutes. Sprinkle with remaining 1 tablespoon parsley just before serving. Serves 6.

Note: Serve with a salad of mixed greens.

Make It Modern: Substitute 4 ounces fresh mushrooms, sliced, for canned mushrooms and 1 tablespoon chopped fresh basil for dried basil.

Chicken Lasagna

INGREDIENTS

- 1 (10½-ounce) can condensed cream of chicken soup, undiluted
- 1 (10½-ounce) can condensed cream of mushroom soup, undiluted
- ½ cup sour cream
- ½ cup Miracle Whip
- Dash garlic powder
- 8 cooked lasagna noodles
- 4 cups chopped cooked chicken
- 1 (10-ounce) package frozen broccoli, thawed and drained
- 4 cups shredded Cheddar cheese

Preheat oven to 350°F.

Combine soups, sour cream, Miracle Whip, and garlic powder in a bowl. Blend together until smooth to make a sauce. Layer ½ each of lasagna noodles, chicken, broccoli, sauce, and cheese in a lightly greased 9x13-inch pan. Repeat layers. Bake 30 minutes. Serves 6–8.

 Make It Modern: Substitute ½ cup cottage cheese or plain yogurt for Miracle Whip.

Chicken Parmigiana

INGREDIENTS

- 1 (16-ounce) package thin spaghetti noodles
- 4 boneless, skinless chicken breast halves, flattened to ¼-inch thick
- ¼ cup all-purpose flour
- 1 cup dry breadcrumbs
- ¾ cup grated Parmesan cheese, divided
- 2 teaspoons dried Italian seasoning
- ¼ teaspoon salt
- 2 eggs, lightly beaten
- 6 tablespoons corn oil
- 1 (8-ounce) package fresh mushrooms, sliced and sautéed in butter
- 1 (24-ounce) jar mushroom marinara sauce, heated
- ¾ cup shredded mozzarella cheese

Preheat oven to 350°F.

Cook spaghetti according to package directions until just tender but not quite done. Place in a lightly greased 2-quart glass baking dish. Coat chicken with flour. Mix together breadcrumbs, ½ cup Parmesan cheese, Italian seasoning, and salt in a large bowl. Dip chicken in eggs; coat with breadcrumb mixture. Heat oil in a saucepan over medium heat; fry each piece of chicken until brown. Place chicken over spaghetti. Top with mushrooms and spaghetti sauce. Top with mozzarella cheese. Sprinkle with remaining ¼ cup Parmesan cheese. Bake, uncovered, 35 minutes or until chicken is no longer pink. Serves 4.

Note: Serve with a green salad and warm garlic bread.

Make It Modern: Consider making the same amount of homemade marinara sauce.

Chicken Tetrazzini

INGREDIENTS

- 4 tablespoons butter, divided
- 2 cloves garlic, minced
- 5 tablespoons all-purpose flour
- 3 cups chicken broth
- ½ cup whipping cream
- ½ teaspoon each salt and pepper
- Pinch ground nutmeg
- ½ pound wide egg noodles, cooked in salted water to barely tender and drained
- ¼ cup minced shallots or onion
- ¼ cup sliced shiitake mushrooms
- ½ pound white mushrooms, sliced
- ¼ teaspoon dried thyme
- 3 tablespoons dry sherry
- 1 cup frozen peas, thawed and divided
- 3 cups cooked chicken, cut into large chunks
- ¼ cup grated Parmesan cheese

Preheat oven to 450°F.

Heat 3 tablespoons butter in a saucepan over medium heat until melted. Add garlic; stir and cook 30 seconds. Add flour; cook while stirring 1 minute. Gradually stir in broth, cream, salt, pepper, and nutmeg until blended. Bring to a boil, stirring constantly; remove sauce from heat. Place noodles in a large bowl. Stir in 1½ cups sauce. Heat remaining 1 tablespoon butter in a large saucepan over medium heat; add shallots, and cook while stirring 1 minute. Add mushrooms and thyme; cook until tender. Add sherry; boil 1 minute. Layer half noodles and ½ cup peas into a lightly greased, shallow 2½-quart glass baking dish. Top with half of the chicken and half of the mushroom mixture. Repeat layers. Pour remaining sauce on top. Top with Parmesan cheese. Bake, uncovered, 25 minutes or until hot and bubbly. Serves 6.

Note: This creamy chicken-pasta hot dish is a snap to prepare with leftover roasted chicken.

Mr. B's Chicken Parmesan

INGREDIENTS

- 2 **eggs, lightly beaten**
- ¾ **cup Italian-seasoned dry breadcrumbs**
- 4 **boneless, skinless chicken breast halves, lightly seasoned with salt**
- 1 **(24-ounce) jar traditional flavor pasta sauce**
- 1 **cup shredded mozzarella cheese**
- ¼ **cup grated Parmesan cheese**
- **Hot cooked pasta**

Preheat oven to 400°F.

Place eggs in a bowl. Place breadcrumbs in another bowl. Dip chicken into egg, then coat with breadcrumbs. Place chicken in a lightly greased 13x9x2-inch glass baking dish. Bake, uncovered, 20 minutes. Pour pasta sauce over chicken. Top with mozzarella cheese, and sprinkle with Parmesan cheese. Bake 15 minutes or until chicken is no longer pink. Serve immediately over hot cooked pasta. Serves 4.

Note: Serve with steamed broccoli or a crisp green salad.

Italian Chicken-Rice Hot Dish

INGREDIENTS

- 1½ cups water
- 1 cup long-grain white rice, uncooked
- 1 (14.5-ounce) can tomatoes, cut up and undrained
- 1 (8-ounce) jar Cheez Whiz
- 1 medium-size onion, chopped
- 1½ teaspoons Italian seasoning, divided
- 1 (2½-pound) broiler-fryer chicken, skinned and cut up
- ⅔ cup grated Parmesan cheese

Preheat oven to 375°F.

Combine water, rice, tomatoes, Cheez Whiz, onion, and 1 teaspoon Italian seasoning in a large bowl; stir well. Spoon rice mixture into a lightly greased 13x9x2-inch glass baking dish. Arrange chicken pieces on top. Sprinkle with remaining ½ teaspoon Italian seasoning. Cover and bake 30 minutes. Uncover, and sprinkle with Parmesan cheese. Bake, uncovered, 20 minutes or until chicken is no longer pink. Serves 4–6.

Note: A green salad will complete this Italian meal.

Cheesy Chicken Enchiladas

INGREDIENTS

1 (8-ounce) jar Cheez Whiz, divided

⅓ cup sour cream

¼ cup chopped green onion

1 teaspoon chili powder

2 cups shredded cooked chicken

6 flour tortillas

Salsa

Preheat oven to 350°F.

Mix together ⅓ cup Cheez Whiz, sour cream, onion, and chili powder in a large bowl. Stir in chicken. Spoon ⅓ cup chicken mixture onto each flour tortilla. Roll up. Place, seam sides down, in a lightly greased 11x13-inch baking dish. Top enchiladas with ½ cup salsa. Bake 25–30 minutes. Microwave remaining Cheese Whiz until hot, and pour over enchiladas. Serve with additional salsa. Serves 6.

 Make It Modern: Substitute 8 ounces freshly grated Cheddar cheese for Cheez Whiz.

Chicken Fajita Hot Dish

INGREDIENTS

1 (8-ounce) box red beans and rice mix

1 (4-ounce) can sliced ripe olives, drained

1 (4-ounce) can diced green chilies, drained

8 boneless, skinless chicken breast tenderloins, lightly seasoned with ground black pepper

2 cups water

1 (14.5-ounce) can diced tomatoes

1 cup shredded Monterey Jack cheese

1 cup crushed tortilla chips

Sour cream

Preheat oven to 350°F.

Spread red beans and rice (minus the seasoning packet) onto bottom of a lightly greased 13x9x2-inch glass baking dish. Top with olives and chilies; then top with chicken. In a saucepan, bring water to a boil over high heat. Add tomatoes and contents of seasoning packet; stir. Pour tomato mixture over top of chicken. Cover; bake 45 minutes. Uncover; sprinkle with cheese and tortilla chips. Bake 5 minutes or until chicken is no longer pink. Serve with sour cream. Serves 4.

Note: A green salad tossed with a vinegar-and-oil dressing will complement this hot dish.

Make It Modern: Use 2 cups diced fresh tomatoes in place of canned tomatoes.

Mexi-Chicken Hot Dish

INGREDIENTS

- 5 tablespoons corn oil
- 12 soft corn tortillas
- 1 cup chopped onion
- 1 cup chopped green bell pepper
- 2 cloves garlic, minced
- 1 (10½-ounce) can condensed cream of chicken soup, undiluted
- 1 (10½-ounce) can condensed cream of mushroom soup, undiluted
- 1 (10-ounce) can tomatoes and green chilies
- ½ teaspoon chili powder
- ¼ teaspoon salt
- 3 cups shredded cooked chicken
- 1 cup shredded Colby cheese
- 1 cup shredded Monterey Jack cheese

Preheat oven to 350°F.

Heat oil in a saucepan over medium heat. Cook tortillas in hot oil a few seconds, one at a time, to soften; drain on paper towels. Cut each tortilla into 4 equal pieces. Reserve 2 tablespoons oil in saucepan. Add onion, bell pepper, and garlic to saucepan; cook while stirring 2 minutes. Combine onion mixture, soups, and next 4 ingredients in a large bowl. Layer half tortilla pieces, half chicken mixture, and half cheeses in a lightly greased 13x9x2-inch baking dish. Repeat layers. Bake 45 minutes or until very hot and bubbly. Serves 6.

Note: Tex-Mex cooking is now enjoyed by many Minnesotans. Serve a lettuce-and-tomato salad with this hot dish.

Tamale-Chicken Hot Dish

INGREDIENTS

- 1 **cup finely crushed corn chips**
- 1 **(15-ounce) can tamales**
- 1 **(10-ounce) can chili with no beans**
- 1½ **cups chopped cooked chicken**
- ½ **(15.25-ounce) can whole kernel corn, undrained**
- 1 **(4-ounce) can chopped green chilies, drained**
- 1 **cup shredded Cheddar cheese**

Preheat oven to 350°F.

Sprinkle corn chips evenly on bottom of a lightly greased 8-inch square baking dish. Unwrap tamales, and layer over corn chips. In a large bowl, mix together chili and next 3 ingredients; spoon chili mixture over tamales. Bake 20 minutes. Sprinkle with cheese, and bake 5 minutes. Serves 4–6.

Note: Serve this hot dish topped with sour cream.

Tex-Mex Chicken and Rice

INGREDIENTS

- 2 cups Minute Rice, uncooked
- 4 boneless, skinless chicken breast halves, cut into bite-size pieces and lightly seasoned with salt
- ½ cup minced onion, cooked in butter 2 minutes
- 2 cloves garlic, minced
- 1 (4-ounce) can diced green chilies, drained
- 1 (14.5-ounce) can diced tomatoes, undrained
- 1 (8-ounce) can tomato sauce
- 1 cup frozen whole-kernel corn, thawed
- ¼ teaspoon salt
- ¼ teaspoon chili powder
- ¼ teaspoon ground cumin

Preheat oven to 350°F.

Spread rice evenly in a lightly greased 2½-quart glass baking dish. Top with chicken. Sprinkle with onion and garlic. Mix together chilies and next 6 ingredients; spoon over last layer. Cover and bake 1 hour. Serves 4.

Note: Serve this hot dish with a crisp green salad.

Broccoli-and-Chicken Hot Dish

INGREDIENTS

- 1 **bunch fresh broccoli, chopped, cooked, and drained**
- 4 **whole boneless, skinless chicken breasts, cooked and chopped**
- 2 **(10½-ounce) cans condensed cream of chicken soup, undiluted**
- 3 **tablespoons mayonnaise**
- 1 **tablespoon fresh lemon juice**
- ¼ **teaspoon curry powder**
- 1 **cup shredded Cheddar cheese**
- 5 **tablespoons grated Parmesan cheese**
- ¼ **cup dry breadcrumbs**

Preheat oven to 350°F.

Place broccoli on bottom of a lightly greased 13x9x2-inch baking dish. Top with chicken. Mix together soup, mayonnaise, lemon juice, and curry powder in a bowl; pour soup mixture over chicken. Sprinkle with cheeses and breadcrumbs. Bake 30 minutes or until very hot. Serves 8.

Note: Serve this hot dish with salad and buttered rolls.

Chicken and Dumplings

INGREDIENTS

- 6 boneless, skinless chicken breast halves
- 1 medium-size onion, chopped
- 2 stalks celery, chopped
- 2 small carrots, sliced
- ½ teaspoon dried sage, crushed
- ⅛ teaspoon dried parsley, crushed
- ⅛ teaspoon ground black pepper
- 2 (14.5-ounce) cans low-sodium chicken broth
- 1 cup all-purpose flour
- 2 teaspoons baking powder
- ¼ teaspoon salt
- 1 tablespoon grated Parmesan cheese
- ½ cup whole milk, mixed with 2 tablespoons corn oil

Preheat oven to 325°F.

Place chicken into a lightly greased 2½-quart glass baking dish. Mix together onion, celery, and carrots in a bowl; spoon onion mixture over chicken. Sprinkle evenly with sage, parsley, and pepper. Pour broth over all. Mix together flour, baking powder, salt, and Parmesan cheese in a bowl. Gradually stir in milk mixture. Mix well to form a dough. Shape dough into 2-inch balls; drop over top of ingredients in baking dish. Cover tightly. Bake 1½ hours. Serves 6.

Note: Chicken and dumplings is a favorite comfort food!

Chicken-Couscous Hot Dish

INGREDIENTS

- 1 cup couscous with sun-dried tomatoes
- 4 boneless, skinless chicken breast halves, seasoned with salt and black pepper
- 2 cloves garlic, finely chopped
- 1 (16-ounce) package button mushrooms, halved and lightly sautéed in 1 teaspoon olive oil
- 1¼ cups water
- 1 tablespoon olive oil
- ¼ teaspoon dried basil

Preheat oven to 350°F.

Spread couscous mixture evenly onto bottom of a lightly greased 10-inch square baking dish. Place chicken over top. Sprinkle garlic over chicken. Top with mushrooms, including liquid. Pour 1¼ cups water over top. Drizzle evenly with olive oil, and sprinkle with basil. Cover and bake 35–40 minutes or until chicken is no longer pink. Serves 4.

Note: Couscous is a granular form of pasta often used like rice.

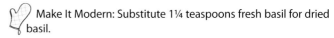 Make It Modern: Substitute 1¼ teaspoons fresh basil for dried basil.

Chicken-Crab Hot Dish

INGREDIENTS

- ¼ cup butter
- ½ cup finely chopped onion
- ¼ cup all-purpose flour
- 1 cup chicken stock
- 1 cup half-and-half
- ½ teaspoon salt
- ¼ teaspoon black pepper
- 2 cups cooked chicken, cut into large pieces
- 1 cup cooked peas
- 1 cup fresh crab meat, picked over
- 1 cup breadcrumbs, mixed with 4 tablespoons melted butter

Preheat oven to 350°F.

Melt butter in a saucepan over medium heat. Add onion; cook while stirring until tender. Stir in flour until blended. Gradually add stock and half-and-half. Stir in salt and pepper. Bring to a boil; cook, stirring constantly, 2 minutes. Layer chicken, peas, and crab meat in a buttered 1½-quart glass baking dish. Top with onion mixture and then breadcrumb mixture. Bake 30 minutes or until browned on top and hot and bubbly. Serves 6.

Note: Serve for a special luncheon along with salad and warm rolls.

Chicken-Stuffing Hot Dish

INGREDIENTS

- 3⅓ cups onion-and-sage bread stuffing mix
- ½ cup butter, melted
- 1 cup water
- 3½ cups diced cooked chicken
- ½ cup chopped onion
- ½ cup chopped celery
- ½ cup mayonnaise
- 2 eggs
- 1½ cups milk
- 1 (10½-ounce) can condensed cream of mushroom soup, mixed with ½ cup whole milk
- 1 cup grated Cheddar cheese

Preheat oven to 325°F.

Combine stuffing mix, butter, and water in a large bowl; spread half stuffing mixture onto bottom of a lightly greased 13x9x2-inch baking dish. Mix together chicken, onion, celery, and mayonnaise in a bowl; spread chicken mixture over stuffing mixture in baking dish. Top with remaining half stuffing mixture. Beat together eggs and 1½ cups milk in a small bowl; pour over all. Cover with aluminum foil, and let stand 20 minutes. Spread soup mixture over top; cover and bake 40 minutes. Sprinkle with cheese; bake 10 minutes. Serves 10.

Note: You can make this hot dish a day ahead; cover and refrigerate overnight. Remove from refrigerator, uncover, and let stand 1 hour before baking.

Jean's Yogurt Chicken

INGREDIENTS

- 1 **cup fine, dry breadcrumbs**
- ¼ **cup grated Parmesan cheese**
- 1½ **tablespoons dried minced onion**
- 1 **teaspoon garlic powder**
- 1 **teaspoon seasoned salt**
- ¼ **teaspoon dried oregano, crushed**
- ¼ **teaspoon dried thyme, crushed**
- 4 **boneless, skinless whole chicken breasts, cut in half lengthwise**
- 2 **cups plain yogurt, divided**
- ¼ **cup butter, melted**
- 2 **teaspoons sesame seeds**
- 2 **(4-ounce) cans sliced mushrooms**
- 6 **plum tomatoes, cut into wedges**
- 1 **(10½-ounce) can condensed cream of chicken soup, undiluted**
- ½ **cup chicken broth**
- 1 **teaspoon lemon juice**
- ½ **teaspoon Worcestershire sauce**
- **Pinch garlic powder**
- **Pinch black pepper**

Preheat oven to 375˚F.

Combine first 7 ingredients in a bowl. Coat chicken with 1 cup yogurt in a separate bowl; dredge chicken in breadcrumb mixture. Place chicken, meaty side up, into a lightly greased 15x10x1-inch baking dish. Drizzle with butter, and sprinkle with sesame seeds. Bake, uncovered, 55 minutes or until chicken is no longer pink. Drain mushrooms; spoon around edge of chicken in dish. Tuck tomato wedges around mushrooms; bake 6 minutes. Stir together soup, remaining 1 cup yogurt, and next 5 ingredients in a saucepan over low heat until thoroughly heated. Spoon yogurt sauce over chicken just before serving. Serves 8.

Note: Jean attended art classes in Minneapolis, and her artistic touch shows in this hot dish! Serve her tangy chicken dish with buttered pasta and a green salad.

Reunion Chicken Hot Dish

INGREDIENTS

- 10 **cups diced cooked chicken**
- 10 **cups chopped celery**
- 2 **whole bunches green onion, including tops, sliced**
- 2 **(4-ounce) cans chopped green chilies, drained**
- 1 **(6-ounce) can pitted ripe olives, drained and sliced**
- 2 **cups slivered almonds**
- ¼ **teaspoon ground black pepper**
- 5 **cups shredded Cheddar cheese, divided**
- 2 **cups mayonnaise**
- 2 **cups sour cream**
- 5 **cups crushed potato chips**

Preheat oven to 350°F.

Combine chicken and next 6 ingredients in a large bowl. Stir in 2 cups cheese. In another bowl, combine mayonnaise and sour cream; stir into chicken mixture until blended. Spoon mixture into 2 lightly greased 13x9x2-inch glass baking dishes. Sprinkle evenly with potato chips. Top with remaining 3 cups cheese. Bake, uncovered, 25–30 minutes or until very hot. Serves 24.

Note: Here's a lot of hot dish to serve—perfect for when the family gets together again. Serve with a relish tray, including sliced fresh tomatoes, carrot sticks, and other fresh vegetables, along with assorted breads and muffins.

Scalloped Chicken Hot Dish

INGREDIENTS

12 slices white bread, cubed

1 cup cracker crumbs

3 cups chicken broth

3 eggs, lightly beaten

1 teaspoon salt

⅛ teaspoon ground black pepper

¾ cup diced celery

¼ cup chopped onion

3 cups cubed cooked chicken

1 (8-ounce) can sliced mushrooms, drained

½ cup cracker crumbs, mixed with 1 tablespoon melted butter

Paprika

Preheat oven to 350°F.

Combine bread cubes and 1 cup cracker crumbs in a large bowl. Gradually stir in broth, eggs, salt, pepper, celery, onion, chicken, and mushrooms. Place chicken mixture into a lightly greased 2-quart baking dish. Sprinkle cracker crumb-butter mixture on top. Bake 1 hour. Sprinkle lightly with paprika. Serves 6.

Note: This dish can be prepared a day ahead of time (without the topping) and refrigerated. Add topping just before baking.

Turkey-Noodle Hot Dish

INGREDIENTS

- 1 **tablespoon butter**
- 1 **tablespoon minced onion**
- 1 **clove garlic, minced**
- 3 **tablespoons all-purpose flour**
- 2½ **cups whole milk**
- 1 **tablespoon chicken-flavor bouillon granules**
- 1 **(8-ounce) package wide egg noodles, cooked according to package directions and drained**
- ½ **cup plain yogurt**
- 2 **cups cubed cooked turkey**
- 2 **cups frozen broccoli cuts, thawed**
- ¼ **teaspoon dried sage**
- 1 **cup shredded Cheddar cheese**

Preheat oven to 375˚F.

Melt butter in a large saucepan over medium heat. Add onion and garlic; cook while stirring 2 minutes. Gradually stir in flour until blended. Stir in milk until smooth. Stir in bouillon granules. Cook and stir until slightly thickened. Stir in noodles and next 4 ingredients. Spoon mixture into a lightly greased 2-quart baking dish. Top with cheese. Cover and bake 30 minutes or until very hot and bubbly. Serves 4–6.

Note: Serve this turkey hot dish with crusty bread and a light fresh fruit salad.

Turkey and Pasta Primavera

INGREDIENTS

- **4 cups (8 ounces) mafalda pasta (mini lasagna noodles)**
- **1½ cups broccoli florets**
- **1 medium-size carrot, sliced**
- **2 medium-size green onions, diagonally sliced**
- **½ medium-size red bell pepper, cut into thin strips**
- **2 (10½-ounce) cans condensed cream of mushroom soup, undiluted**
- **¾ cups water**
- **½ cup Parmesan cheese**
- **2 cups cubed cooked turkey**

Preheat oven to 350°F.

Prepare noodles in a large saucepan according to package directions, adding broccoli, carrot, green onion, and red bell pepper during last 5 minutes of cooking time; drain. Combine soup, water, and cheese in saucepan over high heat; bring to a boil, stirring occasionally. Reduce heat, and stir in noodle mixture and turkey. Place in a lightly greased 11x7-inch baking pan. Bake 30 minutes. Serves 6.

Turkey and Brown Rice

INGREDIENTS

- 1 tablespoon olive oil
- 1 cup chopped onion
- 1 tablespoon chopped garlic
- 1 cup long-grain brown rice, uncooked
- 1 (14.5-ounce) can chicken broth
- ¼ cup water, mixed with ½ teaspoon lemon juice
- ¼ teaspoon dried sage
- 2 tablespoons butter
- 1 (16-ounce) package whole button mushrooms, sliced
- ¼ teaspoon salt
- ¼ teaspoon black pepper
- 3 cups diced cooked turkey
- 1 (10½-ounce) can condensed cream of mushroom soup, mixed with ½ cup milk
- ¼ cup chopped fresh parsley

Preheat oven to 400°F.

Heat oil in a saucepan over medium heat. Add onion; cook while stirring until soft. Add garlic; cook while stirring 1 minute. Stir in rice. Gradually add broth, water mixture, and sage. Bring to a boil. Reduce heat to low; cover and simmer 40 minutes. Melt butter in a small saucepan over medium heat. Add mushrooms; cook while stirring 6 minutes, and drain. Stir in salt and pepper. Spoon rice mixture into a lightly buttered 2-quart shallow baking dish. Top evenly with turkey. Spoon mushroom mixture over turkey. Pour soup mixture over mushrooms. Bake 15 minutes or until bubbly. Cover with aluminum foil, and bake 15 minutes. Top with parsley just before serving. Serves 6.

Note: If desired, substitute shiitake mushrooms, stems removed and sliced, for button mushrooms.

Wild Rice and Turkey Casserole

INGREDIENTS

2 cups diced cooked turkey

2¼ cups boiling water

⅓ cup milk

¼ cup chopped onion

1 (10½-ounce) can condensed cream of mushroom soup, undiluted

1 (6-ounce) package seasoned long-grain and wild rice mix, uncooked

Preheat oven to 350°F.

Mix together all ingredients in an ungreased 2-quart baking dish. Cover and bake 45–60 minutes until rice is tender. Uncover and bake 10–15 minutes or until liquid is absorbed. Serves 4.

Wild Rice-Turkey Casserole

INGREDIENTS

- 3 cups cubed cooked turkey
- 1 cup chopped celery
- 1½ cups cooked long-grain and wild rice
- 1 (10½-ounce) can condensed cream of chicken soup, undiluted
- 2 tablespoons soy sauce
- ¼ teaspoon black pepper
- 1 (4-ounce) can mushrooms, undrained and chopped
- 1 (8-ounce) can sliced water chestnuts, undrained
- 2 bread slices, broken into crumbs
- 1 tablespoon margarine, melted

Preheat oven to 350°F.

Combine turkey and next 7 ingredients in a large bowl; spoon into a lightly greased 9x13-inch baking dish. Top with bread-crumbs, and drizzle with margarine. Bake 1 hour. Serves 4.

Wild Rice-Turkey Hot Dish

INGREDIENTS

- 1 (6-ounce) package long-grain and wild rice mix, cooked according to package directions
- 1 (10½-ounce) can condensed cream of chicken soup, undiluted
- 1 cup water
- 3 cups cubed cooked turkey
- 1 cup chopped celery
- 5 tablespoons chopped onion
- ½ (8-ounce) can sliced water chestnuts, drained
- 1 (4-ounce) can mushroom stems and pieces, drained
- 3 tablespoons soy sauce
- ¼ teaspoon dried thyme
- 1½ cups soft breadcrumbs, mixed with 6 tablespoons melted butter
- 1 tablespoon chopped fresh parsley

Preheat oven to 350°F.

Combine rice and next 9 ingredients in a large bowl. Spoon mixture into a lightly buttered 3-quart baking dish. Top with breadcrumb mixture. Bake 1 hour. Sprinkle with parsley. Serves 8.

Note: This is a good hot dish to make with leftover turkey. Serve with leftover cranberry sauce and steamed fresh broccoli.

Turkey Leftovers Casserole

INGREDIENTS

- **8 cups prepared mashed potatoes**
- **1 (14.5-ounce) can green beans or corn, drained**
- **3 cups diced cooked turkey**
- **1 (12-ounce) jar turkey gravy**
- **1 (6-ounce) package stuffing mix, prepared according to package directions**

Preheat oven to 350°F.

Place mashed potatoes in a lightly greased 9x13-inch pan. Spoon green beans or corn over potatoes. Combine turkey and gravy in a large saucepan over low heat; stir in prepared stuffing mix. Spoon turkey mixture over vegetables. Cover and bake 25–30 minutes. Serves 6.

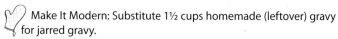 Make It Modern: Substitute 1½ cups homemade (leftover) gravy for jarred gravy.

Turkey-Stuffing Hot Dish

INGREDIENTS

- 1¼ cups water
- ¼ cup butter
- 3½ cups seasoned stuffing crumbs
- 1 (3-ounce) can French fried onions, divided
- 1 (10½-ounce) can condensed cream of celery soup, undiluted
- ¾ cup whole milk
- 1¾ cups cubed cooked turkey
- 1 (10-ounce) package frozen peas, cooked and drained

Preheat oven to 350°F.

Heat water in a medium-size saucepan over medium heat. Add butter; stir until melted. Remove pan from heat. Stir in stuffing crumbs and ½ can French fried onions. Spoon stuffing mixture into a lightly greased 1½-quart round glass baking dish; press stuffing mixture evenly onto bottom and up sides of dish, forming a stuffing shell. Mix together soup, milk, turkey, and peas in a medium-size bowl. Pour turkey mixture into stuffing shell. Bake, covered, 30 minutes or until very hot. Top with remaining ½ can onions. Bake, uncovered, 5 minutes or until onions are golden brown. Serves 4.

Note: Serve this dish with coleslaw and whole-berry cranberry sauce.

Pizza Casserole

INGREDIENTS

- 8 ounces ground turkey
- ½ cup chopped onion
- 3 cups cooked pasta
- 2 ounces thin-sliced pepperoni, chopped
- 2 cups chunky tomato sauce
- 1 teaspoon Italian seasoning
- 1 (4-ounce) can sliced mushrooms
- 3 ounces mozzarella cheese

Preheat oven to 350°F.

Brown ground turkey and onion in a large skillet over medium heat; drain and return to pan. Stir in cooked pasta, pepperoni, tomato sauce, seasoning, and mushrooms. Pour mixture into an ungreased 8-inch square baking dish. Bake 20 minutes. Sprinkle with mozzarella cheese. Bake until cheese is melted. Serves 4.

Turkey-Ham Tetrazzini

INGREDIENTS

- 6 **tablespoons butter**
- 6 **tablespoons all-purpose flour**
- 1 **quart whole milk**
- ¼ **teaspoon salt**
- ¼ **teaspoon ground black pepper**
- 2 **cups diced cooked turkey**
- 2 **cups diced cooked ham**
- ½ **cup diced celery**
- ¼ **cup slivered almonds**
- 1 **tablespoon minced onion**
- 1 **clove garlic, minced**
- 8 **ounces spaghetti, broken, cooked according to package directions, and drained**
- **Grated Parmesan cheese**

Preheat oven to 350°F.

Melt butter in a saucepan over medium heat. Gradually stir in flour; cook while stirring 1 minute. Gradually stir in milk until mixture is smooth. Stir in salt and black pepper. Mix together turkey, ham, and next 5 ingredients in a large bowl. Stir milk mixture into turkey mixture; mix well. Pour mixture into a lightly buttered 13x9x2-inch baking dish. Sprinkle cheese on top. Bake 30 minutes. Let stand 5 minutes before serving. Serves 6 to 8.

Note: Serve this hot dish with a crisp green salad and warm hard rolls.

Turkey Lasagna Hot Dish

INGREDIENTS

- 1 (10½-ounce) can condensed cream of chicken soup, undiluted
- ¾ cup whipping cream
- ½ teaspoon salt
- ½ teaspoon poultry seasoning
- 6 ounces cream cheese
- 1 cup creamed cottage cheese
- ½ cup chopped green onion
- ¼ cup minced fresh parsley
- 2 cups diced cooked turkey
- ½ (16-ounce) package lasagna noodles, cooked according to package directions and drained
- 1 cup soft breadcrumbs, mixed with 2 tablespoons butter

Preheat oven to 350°F.

Combine soup, cream, salt, and poultry seasoning in a large saucepan over medium heat. Combine cream cheese and cottage cheese in a bowl, and beat until smooth; add cream cheese mixture to saucepan. Stir in onion, parsley, and turkey. Place ½ cooked noodles into a buttered 11x7x2-inch glass baking dish. Spoon ½ turkey mixture over noodles. Repeat layers. Top with breadcrumb mixture. Bake 40 minutes or until bubbly in center. Let stand 10 minutes before serving. Serves 6.

Note: This is a great use for leftover turkey.

Turkey Taco Casserole

INGREDIENTS

- 1 **pound ground turkey**
- 1 **small onion, chopped**
- ½ **teaspoon garlic powder**
- 1 **envelope taco seasoning mix**
- 1 **(8-ounce) can tomato sauce**
- 1 **cup sour cream**
- 1 **cup cottage cheese**
- 2 **cups crushed tortilla chips**
- 8 **ounces Monterey Jack cheese, shredded**

Preheat oven to 350°F.

Brown turkey and onion in a skillet over medium heat; drain and return to pan. Stir in garlic powder, taco seasoning mix, and tomato sauce. Combine sour cream and cottage cheese in a bowl. Place ½ crushed tortilla chips in bottom of a lightly greased 2½-quart baking dish. Layer ½ turkey mixture over chips, ½ sour cream mixture, and ½ cheese. Repeat layers. Bake 30 minutes. Serves 4.

 Make It Modern: Garnish with the fresh herbs of your choice.

Turkey Casserole

INGREDIENTS

- **6 cups diced cooked turkey**
- **1 (14.5-ounce) can French-cut green beans, drained**
- **1 cup celery, diced**
- **3 cups croutons or breadcrumbs**
- **½ cup margarine**
- **1 teaspoon salt**
- **¼ teaspoon baking powder**
- **1 teaspoon poultry seasoning**
- **1 egg, lightly beaten**
- **¾ cup milk**
- **1 (10½-ounce) can condensed cream of chicken soup, undiluted**

Preheat oven to 350°F.

Place turkey in a lightly greased 9x13-inch baking dish. Spread green beans over top. Sauté celery and croutons in margarine in a saucepan over medium heat. Stir in salt, baking powder, and poultry seasoning. Stir in egg and milk. Spoon bread mixture over green beans. Spread soup on top. Bake 1 hour. Serves 6.

Make It Modern: Substitute 1½ cups freshly steamed green beans for canned green beans; you can also try shredding the turkey instead of dicing it.

Turkey Tater Hot Dish

INGREDIENTS

- 1 (10½-ounce) can condensed cream of chicken soup, undiluted
- 1 cup milk
- 4 cups diced cooked turkey
- 4 cups frozen mixed vegetables, thawed
- 1 (16-ounce) package frozen Tater Tots
- ½ cup shredded Cheddar cheese

Preheat oven to 375°F.

Mix together soup and milk in a bowl until smooth. Stir in turkey and vegetables. Pour turkey mixture into an ungreased 11x7-inch baking dish. Arrange tater tots on top. Bake 40 minutes. Sprinkle cheese on top. Bake 5–10 minutes or until cheese is melted. Let stand 10 minutes before serving. Serves 6.

Beef

3-Bean Beef Hot Dish

INGREDIENTS

- 1 **pound ground beef**
- ½ **pound bacon, chopped**
- 1 **cup chopped onion**
- ½ **cup ketchup**
- 1 **teaspoon salt**
- 2 **teaspoons vinegar**
- ½ **cup brown sugar**
- 2 **teaspoons prepared mustard**
- 1 **(15-ounce) can butter beans, drained**
- 1 **(16-ounce) can baked beans**
- 2 **(16-ounce) cans kidney beans, drained**

Preheat oven to 350°F.

Cook beef, bacon, and onion in a large skillet over medium heat until beef is no longer pink; drain and return to skillet. Stir in ketchup and next 7 ingredients. Pour mixture into a lightly greased 3½-quart baking dish. Cover and bake 40 minutes. Serves 6.

Note: This is a main dish hot dish. To make a baked bean side dish, just leave out the ground beef.

Baked Chili Hot Dish

INGREDIENTS

1 **pound ground beef**

1 **cup chopped onion**

1 **large green bell pepper, chopped**

3 **large cloves garlic, minced**

1 **(16-ounce) can kidney beans, drained**

1 **(15-ounce) can whole-kernel corn, drained**

1 **(16-ounce) can diced tomatoes, undrained**

1 **(4-ounce) can chopped green chilies, undrained**

2 **teaspoons chili powder**

1 **teaspoon ground cumin**

¾ **teaspoon salt, divided**

1 **cup all-purpose flour**

2 **teaspoons baking powder**

1 **cup yellow cornmeal**

¼ **cup whole milk**

¼ **cup sour cream**

1 **large egg, lightly beaten**

Preheat oven to 400 °F.

Cook beef, onion, and bell pepper in a large skillet over medium heat until beef is no longer pink; drain and return to skillet. Add garlic; cook while stirring 1 minute. Stir in kidney beans, next 5 ingredients, and ½ teaspoon salt. Bring to a boil. Reduce heat; cover and simmer 15 minutes, stirring occasionally. Spoon beef mixture into a lightly greased 13x9x2-inch baking dish. Combine flour, baking powder, remaining ¼ teaspoon salt, and cornmeal in a bowl until blended. Combine milk, sour cream, and egg in a separate bowl until blended. Gradually add milk mixture to flour mixture, stirring only to moisten. Drop by teaspoonfuls on top of beef mixture in baking dish. Bake, uncovered, 20 minutes or until cornbread topping is light golden brown. Serves 8.

Note: Offer additional sour cream when serving this corn-bread-topped chili. Serve with a crisp salad.

Beef 'n' Beans Hot Dish

INGREDIENTS

- **3 pounds ground beef**
- **1½ cups chopped onion**
- **½ cup chopped celery**
- **3 cloves garlic, minced**
- **2 teaspoons beef bouillon granules, dissolved in 1 cup boiling water**
- **2 (28-ounce) cans baked beans with molasses**
- **1¼ teaspoons salt**
- **½ teaspoon ground black pepper**
- **½ teaspoon Worcestershire sauce**
- **½ pound sliced bacon, crisply cooked and crumbled**

Preheat oven to 375°F.

Cook beef, onion, and celery in a large skillet over medium heat until beef is no longer pink; drain and return to skillet. Add garlic; cook while stirring 1 minute. Add beef bouillon mixture and next 4 ingredients. Mix well. Spoon beef mixture into a lightly greased 3-quart baking dish. Cover and bake 1 hour. Stir in ½ bacon, and sprinkle remaining ½ bacon on top. Serves 12.

Note: Serve this beefy hot dish with a salad and warm crusty bread.

Beef 'n' Biscuits Hot Dish

INGREDIENTS

- 1 **pound ground beef**
- ½ **cup chopped onion**
- 1 **(10½-ounce) can condensed cream of mushroom soup, undiluted**
- 1 **(8-ounce) package cream cheese, cut up**
- 1 **(15-ounce) can whole-kernel corn, drained**
- ¼ **cup chopped pimientos**
- ¼ **teaspoon salt**
- **Pinch ground black pepper**
- 1 **(7.5-ounce) can refrigerated buttermilk biscuits**

Preheat oven to 375°F.

Cook beef in a large skillet until no longer pink; drain and return to skillet. Add onion; cook while stirring until tender. Add soup and cream cheese, stirring until cheese is melted. Add corn, pimientos, salt, and black pepper; mix lightly. Pour beef mixture into a lightly greased 1½-quart baking dish. Separate dough into 10 biscuits; cut each one in half crosswise. Place each half, cut side down, around edges of baking dish. Bake about 25 minutes or until biscuits are browned. Serves 6.

Note: Serve a mixed green salad with this hearty meal.

 Make It Modern: Consider substituting your favorite homemade biscuit recipe instead of using canned biscuits.

Biscuit-Topped Beef Hot Dish

INGREDIENTS

- 1 **pound ground beef**
- 1 **medium-size onion, chopped**
- 2 **cloves garlic, chopped**
- ¾ **cup water**
- ½ **teaspoon salt**
- ¼ **teaspoon black pepper**
- 1 **(8-ounce) can tomato sauce**
- 1 **(6-ounce) can tomato paste**
- ½ **(16-ounce) package frozen mixed vegetables, thawed**
- 2 **cups shredded mozzarella cheese, divided**
- 1 **(16-ounce) can refrigerated buttermilk biscuits**
- 1 **tablespoon butter, melted**
- ½ **teaspoon dried oregano leaves, crushed**

Preheat oven to 375°F.

Cook beef and onion in a large skillet over medium heat until beef is no longer pink; drain and return to skillet. Add garlic; cook while stirring 1 minute. Stir in water, salt, pepper, tomato sauce, and tomato paste; bring to a boil. Reduce heat and simmer 15 minutes, stirring often. Stir in vegetables and 1½ cups cheese. Spoon beef mixture into a lightly greased 2-quart glass baking dish. Separate dough into 8 biscuits. Separate each biscuit into 2 layers. Place biscuits near outer edge of meat mixture, overlapping slightly. Sprinkle remaining ½ cup cheese in center and around edge. Gently brush biscuits with melted butter and sprinkle with oregano. Bake about 25 minutes or until biscuits are golden brown. Serves 6.

A crisp green salad will complete this tasty, easy-to-prepare, Italian-flavored meal.

Cheesy Spaghetti Hot Dish

INGREDIENTS

- 1 **tablespoon butter**
- 1 **cup chopped onion**
- 1 **cup chopped green bell pepper**
- 1 **pound ground beef**
- 1 **(28-ounce) can tomatoes, chopped and undrained**
- 1 **(4-ounce) can mushroom stems and pieces, drained**
- 1 **(3.8-ounce) can sliced ripe olives, drained**
- 1½ **teaspoons dried oregano**
- 12 **ounces spaghetti, cooked according to package directions and drained**
- 2 **cups shredded Cheddar cheese, divided**
- 1 **(10½-ounce) can condensed cream of mushroom soup, mixed with ¼ cup water**
- ¼ **cup grated Parmesan cheese**

Preheat oven to 350˚F.

Melt butter in a large saucepan over medium heat. Add onion and green bell pepper; cook while stirring until soft. Add beef, and cook until no longer pink; drain, reserving 1 tablespoon drippings, and return beef to pan. Stir in tomatoes, mushrooms, olives, and oregano. Simmer, uncovered, 10 minutes. Place ½ cooked spaghetti in a lightly greased 13x9x2-inch baking dish. Top with ½ beef mixture. Sprinkle with 1 cup Cheddar cheese. Repeat layers. Pour soup mixture over all. Sprinkle with Parmesan cheese. Bake, uncovered, 30–35 minutes or until hot and bubbly. Serves 8.

Note: A crisp green salad and warm garlic bread go well with this spaghetti hot dish.

Corned Beef Hot Dish

INGREDIENTS

- 2 cups elbow macaroni
- 1 tablespoon butter
- 1 (12-ounce) can corned beef, chopped
- ¼ pound Cheddar cheese, shredded
- ½ cup chopped onion
- 1 (10½-ounce) can condensed cream of chicken soup, undiluted
- 1 cup whole milk
- ½ cup finely chopped celery
- Potato chips

Preheat oven to 350°F.

Cook macaroni 3 minutes less than package directions; drain. Place in a large bowl; add butter, and stir. Add corned beef and next 5 ingredients; mix well. Spoon corned beef mixture into a lightly greased 2½-quart baking dish. Crumble enough potato chips to cover top. Bake, uncovered, 1 hour or until very hot and bubbly. Serves 4.

Note: This hot dish comes from Perley, Minnesota's 100th-anniversary edition of the Kirkebo Lutheran Church cookbook.

Cotton Lake Hot Dish

INGREDIENTS

- 1 tablespoon corn oil
- 1 medium-size onion, chopped
- ½ medium-size green bell pepper, chopped
- 1 pound ground beef
- ¼ teaspoon salt
- Pinch ground black pepper
- 2 (8-ounce) cans tomato sauce
- ¼ pound American cheese, cut up
- 3½ cups elbow macaroni, cooked 3 minutes less than package directions and drained

Preheat oven to 350°F.

Heat oil in a saucepan over medium heat; add onion and bell pepper, and cook while stirring until soft. Add ground beef, and cook until no longer pink; drain, reserving 1 tablespoon drippings, and return beef mixture to pan. Stir in salt, pepper, tomato sauce, and cheese; cook 2 minutes. Combine beef mixture and macaroni in a lightly greased 2½-quart glass baking dish. Bake, uncovered, 30–35 minutes or until hot and bubbly. Serves 4.

Note: Theresa's family spent many summers at their cottage on Cotton Lake, located near Detroit Lakes, Minnesota. When they didn't have any real luck fishing, they turned to this hot dish—along with a healing dessert!

Simple Pasta Hot Dish

INGREDIENTS

- 1 **pound ground beef**
- 5 **cups cooked elbow macaroni or rotini pasta**
- 1 **(24-ounce) jar spaghetti sauce**
- ½ **cup grated Parmesan cheese**
- 1 **(8-ounce) package shredded mozzarella cheese**

Preheat oven to 375°F.

Cook beef in a large saucepan over medium heat until beef is no longer pink; drain and return to pan. Stir in pasta, spaghetti sauce, and Parmesan cheese. Spoon beef mixture into a lightly greased 13x9x2-inch baking dish. Top with mozzarella cheese. Bake, uncovered, 20 minutes. Serves 4.

Note: This is so easy to prepare. Serve it with a crisp salad.

String Hot Dish

INGREDIENTS

- 1 **pound ground beef**
- 1 **medium-size onion, chopped**
- ¼ **cup chopped green bell pepper**
- ⅔ **(24-ounce) jar spaghetti sauce**
- 8 **ounces spaghetti, cooked according to package directions and drained**
- 6 **tablespoons Parmesan cheese**
- 2 **eggs, lightly beaten**
- 2 **teaspoons butter**
- 1 **cup cottage cheese**
- ½ **cup shredded mozzarella cheese**

Preheat oven to 350°F.

Cook beef, onion, and green bell pepper in a saucepan over medium-high heat until beef is no longer pink; drain and return beef mixture to pan. Stir in spaghetti sauce; mix well. Mix together hot spaghetti noodles, Parmesan cheese, eggs, and butter in a large bowl. Spoon spaghetti noodle mixture onto bottom of a lightly greased 13x9x2-inch glass baking dish. Spread cottage cheese over top. Pour beef mixture over cottage cheese. Sprinkle evenly with mozzarella cheese. Bake, uncovered, 20 minutes or until cheese melts. Serves 6.

Note: Salad and warm garlic bread go well with this string (spaghetti) hot dish.

Good Beef 'n' Rice Hot Dish

INGREDIENTS

- **1 pound ground beef**
- **1 large onion, chopped**
- **½ cup long-grain white rice, uncooked**
- **1 teaspoon salt**
- **Pinch ground black pepper**
- **1½ cups tomato juice**

Preheat oven to 375°F.

Cook beef and onion in a large saucepan over medium heat until beef is no longer pink; drain, reserving 1 tablespoon drippings in pan, and return beef mixture to pan. Stir in rice, salt, pepper, and tomato juice; mix well. Spoon beef mixture into a lightly greased 2½-quart baking dish. Cover and bake 1 hour. Serves 6.

Note: This is a hot dish Theresa would put in the oven when her family was in a hurry to go fishing. She served it with green salad, canned corn, and bread—buttered, of course.

Hamburger Wild Rice Hot Dish

INGREDIENTS

- 1 **cup long-grain and wild rice, washed**
- **4 cups boiling water**
- 1½ **pound ground beef**
- ¼ **cup chopped onion**
- 1 **(10½-ounce) can condensed cream of chicken soup, undiluted**
- 1 **(10½-ounce) can condensed cream of mushroom soup, undiluted**
- 1 **(4-ounce) can mushroom stems and pieces, drained**
- 1 **small can water chestnuts, drained and sliced**
- 2 **beef bouillon cubes, mixed with 2 cups boiling water**
- **Salt**
- **Ground black pepper**

Preheat oven to 350°F.

Place rice in a saucepan, and cover with 4 cups boiling water. Simmer 5 minutes. Remove from heat, and let stand 15 minutes; drain. Cook beef and onion in a large skillet over medium heat until beef is no longer pink; drain. Combine rice, beef mixture, and next 5 ingredients in a lightly greased 11x7-inch baking dish. Season with salt and pepper to taste. Cover and bake 45 minutes. Remove cover and bake 45 minutes. Serves 4.

Millie's Wild Rice Hot Dish

INGREDIENTS

- 2 slices bread, toasted
- Whole milk
- 1 egg, lightly beaten
- ½ pound ground beef
- ½ pound ground lean pork
- 1 medium-size onion, grated
- Salt and ground black pepper
- 2 tablespoons butter
- 1 cup long-grain and wild rice, washed
- Water
- 1 cup chopped celery
- ½ medium-size green bell pepper, diced
- 1 cup sliced mushrooms
- 1 (10½-ounce) can condensed cream of mushroom soup, undiluted
- ¼ cup grated Parmesan cheese

Preheat oven to 350°F.

Crumble toast into enough milk to cover in a large bowl; soak well. Add egg, meat, onion, salt, and pepper to taste. Form meat mixture into meatballs. Melt butter in a saucepan over medium heat. Add meatballs; brown lightly. Meanwhile, place rice and enough water to cover in a deep saucepan over high heat. Stir in celery, green bell pepper, and salt to taste. Bring to a boil; reduce heat, and simmer until rice is almost tender. Stir in mushrooms, soup, ½ soup can water, and cheese; mix well. Place rice mixture into a lightly greased 2½-quart baking dish. Arrange meatballs over rice, pressing gently into rice mixture. Cover and bake 45 minutes or until rice is tender and meat is no longer pink. Serves 6.

Note: Cousin Mildred Distad taught music most of her life. She retired in Moorhead, Minnesota, where she loved trying new hot dishes—this is one of them.

Spanish Rice Hot Dish

INGREDIENTS

- 1 pound ground beef, seasoned with ¼ teaspoon salt and pinch ground black pepper
- 2 tablespoons olive oil or margarine
- 1 medium-size onion, chopped
- ½ cup chopped green bell pepper
- 1 cup diced celery
- 2 (8-ounce) cans tomato sauce
- 1 teaspoon salt
- 1 cup long-grain white rice, cooked according to package directions

Preheat oven to 375°F.

Cook beef in a saucepan over medium heat until no longer pink; drain. Place beef in a lightly greased 2-quart baking dish. Heat oil in same saucepan over medium heat; stir in onion, green bell pepper, and celery, and cook 5 minutes. Add tomato sauce and salt. Cover; simmer 10 minutes, stirring occasionally. Spoon tomato sauce mixture on top of beef in baking dish. Add cooked rice; stir until well blended. Bake, uncovered, 25 minutes. Serves 4.

Note: Spanish rice is an old favorite hot dish. Serve it with a tossed green salad.

Spanish Rice with Mushrooms

INGREDIENTS

- ¼ cup olive oil, divided
- 1 (8-ounce) package beef-flavor rice mix, uncooked
- 1 pound ground beef
- ½ cup chopped onion
- ¼ cup diced green bell pepper
- ¼ cup sliced stuffed olives
- 2 (14.5-ounce) cans stewed tomatoes
- 1 (8-ounce) can sliced mushrooms, drained
- 1 cup water
- Salt and black pepper

Preheat oven to 350°F.

Heat 3 tablespoons oil in a saucepan over medium heat; add rice. (Do not add the seasoning mix packet yet.) Stir and cook until golden. Spoon rice into a lightly greased 2-quart baking dish. Sprinkle seasoning mix packet over rice. Heat remaining 1 tablespoon oil in saucepan. Add beef, onion, and green bell pepper to pan. Cook over medium heat until beef is no longer pink; drain. Spoon beef mixture on top of rice in baking dish. Add olives, tomatoes, mushrooms, and 1 cup water. Mix well. Cover and bake 45 minutes or until rice is tender. Uncover and fluff mixture with a fork. Season with salt and pepper to taste. Serves 6.

Note: This hot dish is versatile. Omit the olives and increase the green bell pepper, if desired. Serve with a green salad and the bread of your choice.

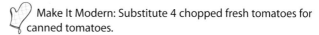 Make It Modern: Substitute 4 chopped fresh tomatoes for canned tomatoes.

Wild Rice-Beef Hot Dish

INGREDIENTS

- 3 cups water
- 1 cup long-grain and wild rice, rinsed and uncooked
- 1 teaspoon salt
- 2 tablespoons butter, divided
- 1 pound ground beef
- 3 cups sliced fresh mushrooms
- 2 stalks celery, chopped
- ½ cup chopped onion
- 1 (10½-ounce) can cream of mushroom soup, undiluted
- 1¼ cups water
- ⅛ teaspoon ground black pepper
- 1 tablespoon soy sauce

Preheat oven to 375˚F.

Bring 3 cups water to a boil in a saucepan over high heat. Add rice and salt; reduce heat, and simmer 40 minutes. Meanwhile, melt 1 tablespoon butter in a large saucepan over medium heat. Add beef, and cook until no longer pink; drain and remove beef to a large bowl. Melt remaining 1 tablespoon butter in saucepan. Add mushrooms, celery, and onion; cook while stirring 3 minutes. Add rice to beef in large bowl; stir in mushroom mixture and next 4 ingredients; mix well. Spoon rice mixture into a lightly greased 13x9x2-inch glass baking dish. Bake 55 minutes. Serves 6.

Note: Minnesota is famous for genuine wild rice. Serve this hot dish with a crisp green salad and warm crusty bread—buttered, of course.

Baked Beef Stew

INGREDIENTS

- 2 tablespoons corn oil
- 2 pounds boneless beef chuck, cut into 2-inch chunks and lightly seasoned with salt and pepper
- 2 medium-size onions, chopped
- 3 tablespoons all-purpose flour
- 2 cups beef broth
- 3 cloves garlic, minced
- ¼ teaspoon dried thyme
- ¼ teaspoon dried marjoram
- 2 potatoes, peeled and cut into chunks
- 1 (8-ounce) package fresh mushrooms, cooked in butter 2 minutes and drained
- 1 cup sliced carrots and ½ cup sliced celery, cooked in 1 tablespoon butter until tender

Preheat oven to 325°F.

Heat oil in a saucepan over medium heat. Add seasoned beef; stir and cook until brown. Place in a lightly greased 3½-quart glass baking dish. Add onion to saucepan; cook while stirring until light brown, and place in baking dish. Gradually stir flour into remaining oil in saucepan until blended. Gradually stir in broth; cook while stirring until mixture boils and thickens. Add garlic and next 4 ingredients; mix well, and pour into baking dish. Cover and bake 2½ hours. Stir in carrot-and-celery mixture; cover and bake 20 minutes. Serves 6.

Note: Stew is usually cooked on top of the stove, so try this method for a change. Serve stew in bowls along with rolls, or spoon it over hot white rice alongside a tossed salad.

Stay-in-Bed Stew

INGREDIENTS

- 2 pounds stew meat
- 1 cup sliced carrots
- 2 cups chopped onion
- 2 large potatoes, diced
- 1 cup peas
- 1 cup chopped celery
- 1 (10½-ounce) can condensed cream of mushroom soup, undiluted
- 1 (10½-ounce) can tomato soup, mixed with ½ soup can water
- 1 teaspoon salt
- Dash pepper

Preheat oven to 300°F.

Cut meat into small pieces, and place it in an ovenproof pan. Stir in carrots and next 8 ingredients. Cover pan and bake 4 hours.

Chow Mein Hot Dish

INGREDIENTS

- 1 **pound ground beef**
- ½ **cup chopped celery**
- ¼ **cup chopped onion**
- ¾ **cup Minute Rice, uncooked**
- 1¼ **cups boiling water**
- ½ **teaspoon salt**
- 1 **(10½-ounce) can condensed chicken and rice soup, undiluted**
- 1 **(4-ounce) can sliced mushrooms, drained**
- 1 **tablespoon brown sugar**
- 2 **tablespoons soy sauce**
- 1 **teaspoon margarine**
- 1½ **cups chow mein noodles**

Preheat oven to 350°F.

Cook beef, celery, and onion in a large skillet over medium heat until beef is no longer pink; drain. Place rice in a lightly greased 2-quart baking dish. Pour boiling water over rice. Stir in beef mixture and next 6 ingredients. Cover and bake 30 minutes. Uncover, and stir; bake, uncovered, 30 minutes. Stir in chow mein noodles just before serving. Serves 4.

Note: This tasty hot dish is so easy to prepare. Thanks, Evie!

Baked Rotini

INGREDIENTS

- ½ pound rotini pasta
- 1 pound ground beef
- 1 cup chopped onion
- 1 green bell pepper, chopped
- 1 (28-ounce) can tomatoes
- 1 (6-ounce) can tomato paste
- 1 (4-ounce) can mushrooms, drained
- 1 teaspoon salt
- ½ teaspoon dried basil
- ½ teaspoon dried oregano
- ¼ teaspoon minced garlic
- ¼ teaspoon black pepper
- 2 cups mozzarella cheese

Preheat oven to 350°F.

Prepare pasta according to package directions; drain. Cook beef, onion, and green bell pepper in a large skillet over medium heat until beef is no longer pink; drain and return to skillet. Stir in tomatoes, tomato paste, mushrooms, and next 5 ingredients. Simmer 20 minutes. Stir in pasta. Pour beef mixture into a lightly greased 9x13-inch pan. Top with mozzarella cheese. Bake 35–40 minutes. Serves 4.

 Make It Modern: Substitute 1 cup provolone for mozzarella.

Beef-Corn Lasagna

INGREDIENTS

- 1 **pound ground beef**
- ½ **cup finely chopped onion**
- 1 **(15-ounce) can whole-kernel corn, drained**
- 2 **cloves garlic, minced**
- ½ **teaspoon salt**
- 1 **(15-ounce) can tomato sauce**
- 1 **cup picante sauce**
- 1 **tablespoon chili powder**
- 1½ **teaspoons ground cumin**
- 1 **(16-ounce) carton low-fat cottage cheese**
- 2 **eggs, lightly beaten**
- ¼ **cup grated Parmesan cheese**
- 1 **teaspoon dried oregano, crushed**
- 12 **corn tortillas**
- 1 **cup shredded Cheddar cheese**

Preheat oven to 375°F.

Cook beef and onion in a large skillet over medium heat until beef is no longer pink; drain and return to skillet. Add corn, garlic, salt, tomato sauce, picante sauce, chili powder, and cumin. Simmer 5 minutes, stirring often. Mix together cottage cheese, eggs, Parmesan cheese, and oregano in a bowl. Place 6 tortillas on bottom and up sides of a lightly greased 13x9x2-inch glass baking dish, overlapping as necessary. Top with ½ beef mixture. Spoon cottage cheese mixture over meat layer. Place remaining 6 tortillas over cottage cheese, overlapping as necessary. Top with remaining ½ beef mixture. Bake 35 minutes or until bubbly. Sprinkle with Cheddar cheese. Let stand 10 minutes before serving. Serves 8.

Note: Serve this Tex-Mex lasagna with a green salad.

Beef-Rigatoni Hot Dish

INGREDIENTS

- 1 tablespoon olive oil
- ½ pound ground beef, lightly seasoned with salt
- 1 small onion, chopped
- 2½ cups rigatoni pasta, cooked according to package directions and drained
- 1 (16-ounce) jar chunky salsa
- 1 (15-ounce) can black beans, drained
- 1 cup frozen whole-kernel corn
- ½ cup shredded Monterey Jack cheese, mixed with ½ cup shredded Cheddar cheese
- 2 plum tomatoes, thinly sliced
- Garnish: Chopped fresh flat-leaf parsley

Preheat oven to 350°F.

Heat oil in a large skillet over medium heat. Add beef and onion; cook while stirring until beef is no longer pink; drain and return to skillet. Add pasta, salsa, black beans, and corn; mix well. Spoon ½ beef mixture into a lightly greased 4-quart baking dish. Sprinkle with ½ cheese mixture. Layer remaining ½ beef mixture, tomatoes, and remaining ½ cheese mixture. Cover and bake 40 minutes. Garnish, if desired. Serves 4–6.

Note: Serve this hot dish with salad and garlic bread.

Classic Italian Lasagna

INGREDIENTS

- ½ **pound ground beef**
- ½ **pound ground lean pork**
- ¾ **cup chopped onion**
- 3 **cloves garlic, crushed**
- 1 **(28-ounce) can whole tomatoes, undrained**
- 2 **(6-ounce) cans tomato paste**
- ½ **teaspoon salt**
- 1 **teaspoon dried basil**
- ½ **teaspoon dried oregano**
- ¼ **teaspoon crushed dried red pepper**
- 16 **lasagna noodles, uncooked**
- 1¾ **cup ricotta or cottage cheese**
- 2 **cups shredded mozzarella cheese, divided**
- ¼ **cup grated Parmesan cheese**
- ¼ **cup chopped fresh parsley**
- 2 **eggs, lightly beaten**
- ¼ **teaspoon ground black pepper**

Preheat oven to 350°F.

Cook beef, pork, onion, and garlic in a large skillet over medium heat until meat is no longer pink; drain, and return to skillet. Add tomatoes, tomato paste, salt, basil, oregano, and red pepper; simmer, covered, 20 minutes. Meanwhile, cook lasagna according to package directions; drain. Lay noodles flat on aluminum foil to cool. Stir together ricotta cheese, 1 cup mozzarella cheese, Parmesan cheese, parsley, eggs, and black pepper in a bowl. Spread 1 cup meat mixture on bottom of a lightly greased 13x9x2-inch baking dish. Arrange 4 lasagna noodles lengthwise over meat mixture, overlapping edges. Layer ⅓ cheese mixture and 1 cup meat mixture on top of noodles. Repeat layers twice, beginning with noodles. Top with 1 cup mozzarella cheese. Cover with aluminum foil. Bake 30 minutes or until hot and bubbly. Remove foil; bake 10 minutes. Let stand 10 minutes before cutting. Serves 6.

Note: Salad and French bread complete this meal.

Lasagna

INGREDIENTS

- 8 lasagna noodles, uncooked
- 2 pounds ground beef
- 1 (28-ounce) can tomatoes
- 1 (15-ounce) can tomato sauce
- 2 (1.37-ounce) packets Thick-&-Zesty Spaghetti Sauce Mix
- 12 ounces cottage cheese
- 1 egg, lightly beaten
- 8 ounces mozzarella cheese
- Parmesan cheese

Preheat oven to 325°F.

Cook lasagna noodles according to package directions; drain. Cook beef in a large skillet over medium heat until no longer pink; drain and return to skillet. Stir in next 3 ingredients; simmer 5 minutes. Mix together cottage cheese and egg in a bowl. Place 4 noodles in a lightly greased 9x13-inch baking dish. Layer ½ beef mixture, ½ cottage cheese mixture, then ½ mozzarella cheese. Repeat layers once. Sprinkle Parmesan cheese on top. Bake 50–60 minutes. Cool 10 minutes before serving. Serves 8.

Pizza Hot Dish

INGREDIENTS

- 1 **pound ground beef**
- 1 **teaspoon salt**
- ¼ **teaspoon pepper**
- 1 **(16-ounce) box radiatore (pasta nuggets)**
- 1 **(15-ounce) can tomato sauce**
- ½ **teaspoon basil**
- 1 **(24-ounce) jar spaghetti sauce**
- ½ **teaspoon garlic salt**
- ¼ **teaspoon oregano**
- 16 **ounces shredded mozzarella cheese, divided**

Preheat oven to 350°F.

Cook beef with salt and pepper in a large saucepan over medium heat until beef is no longer pink; drain and return beef mixture to pan. Cook pasta nuggets according to package directions; drain. Combine beef, pasta, tomato sauce, next 4 ingredients, and ½ cheese in an ungreased 9x13-inch baking dish; bake 30 minutes. Sprinkle with remaining ½ cheese, and bake 30 minutes. Serves 4.

Ravioli Hot Dish

INGREDIENTS

- 1 **pound ground beef, lightly seasoned with salt**
- 2 **tablespoons finely chopped onion**
- 1 **(24-ounce) jar spaghetti sauce**
- 1 **(25-ounce) package frozen cheese ravioli, thawed**
- 1½ **cups shredded mozzarella cheese**

Preheat oven to 425°F.

Cook beef and onion in a saucepan over medium heat until beef is no longer pink; drain. In a lightly greased 11x7x2-inch glass baking dish, layer 1 cup spaghetti sauce, ½ ravioli, ½ beef mixture, and ½ cheese. Next, layer 1 cup spaghetti sauce, remaining ½ ravioli, and remaining ½ beef mixture. Pour remaining spaghetti sauce on top. Bake, uncovered, 30–35 minutes. Top with remaining ½ cheese; bake until cheese is melted. Serves 4.

Note: A salad and garlic bread will go nicely with this ravioli hot dish that's almost lasagna!

Stuffed Jumbo Shells

INGREDIENTS

1½ pounds ground beef

1 chopped onion

½ cup milk

1 egg, lightly beaten

3 slices moist bread

1 clove garlic, chopped

1 (12-ounce) box jumbo pasta shells

1 (24-ounce) jar spaghetti sauce

16 ounces mozzarella cheese

Preheat oven to 350°F.

Cook beef and onion in a large saucepan over medium heat until beef is no longer pink; drain and return beef mixture to pan. Stir in milk and next 3 ingredients. Cook pasta shells according to package directions; drain. Filled prepared shells with beef mixture. Pour small amount of spaghetti sauce into bottom of a lightly greased 9x13-inch pan. Put shells in pan, and cover with remaining sauce. Top with mozzarella, and bake 20–30 minutes. Serves 4–6.

Ziti 'n' Meatballs Hot Dish

INGREDIENTS

- 1½ pounds ground beef
- 1 pound hot Italian link sausage, casings removed, crumbled
- 2 tablespoons minced yellow onion
- 2 cloves garlic, minced
- 1 (10-ounce) package frozen chopped spinach, thawed
- ½ cup plain dry breadcrumbs
- 1 cup grated Parmesan cheese, divided
- 2 eggs, lightly beaten
- ½ teaspoon salt
- ¼ teaspoon ground black pepper
- 6 cups prepared spaghetti sauce
- 1 (16-ounce) package ziti pasta
- 8 ounces mozzarella cheese, cut up
- 15 ounces ricotta cheese

Preheat oven to 375°F.

Combine beef, sausage, onion, garlic, spinach, breadcrumbs, ½ cup Parmesan cheese, eggs, salt, and pepper in a large bowl. Mix well and shape into 4 dozen meatballs. Pour spaghetti sauce into a deep saucepan; bring to a simmer, and place meatballs into sauce. Cover and simmer 35 minutes. Meanwhile, cook ziti according to package directions. Drain and place into a lightly greased 4-quart baking dish. Add sauce with meatballs; stir. Cover with aluminum foil. Bake 25 minutes. Stir in mozzarella cheese. Combine ricotta and remaining ½ cup Parmesan cheese; drop by rounded tablespoonfuls over top. Cover and bake 15 minutes. Serves 12.

Note: You can vary the amount of meatballs by enlarging or reducing their size. Serve this dish with a tossed salad.

Ali's Beef Enchiladas

INGREDIENTS

- 1 **pound ground beef, lightly seasoned with salt and ground black pepper**
- ½ **cup chopped onion**
- 1 **cup picante sauce, divided**
- ¾ **teaspoon ground cumin**
- **Corn oil**
- 12 **corn tortillas**
- ¾ **cup shredded Cheddar cheese**
- ¾ **cup shredded Monterey Jack cheese**

Preheat oven to 350°F.

Cook beef and onion in a large skillet over medium heat until beef is no longer pink; drain and return to skillet. Stir in ½ cup picante sauce and cumin. Pour oil to ½-inch deep in a saucepan over medium-high heat. Quickly fry each tortilla in oil to soften, 2 seconds on each side; drain on paper towels. Spoon ¼ cup beef mixture down center of each tortilla; roll and place, seam side down, into a lightly greased 13x9x2-inch baking dish. Spoon remaining ½ cup picante sauce evenly over enchiladas. Top evenly with cheeses. Bake 15 minutes or until very hot. Serves 6.

Note: If desired, substitute flour tortillas, which need no frying, for corn tortillas. Serve with a lettuce-and-avocado salad.

Mexican Pasta Hot Dish

INGREDIENTS

- 1 **pound pasta**
- 1 **pound ground beef**
- 1 **(28-ounce) can diced tomatoes**
- ¾ **cup salsa**
- 1 **packet taco seasoning mix**
- 2 **teaspoons ground cumin**
- 1 **tablespoon chili powder**
- ½ **teaspoon cayenne pepper**
- 1 **(15-ounce) can whole-kernel corn, drained**
- 1 **cup grated Cheddar cheese**

Preheat oven to 350°F.

Cook pasta according to package directions; drain. Cook beef in a large skillet over medium heat until no longer pink; drain and return to skillet. Stir in tomatoes, salsa, taco seasoning, cumin, chili powder, and cayenne pepper until blended. Stir in corn and pasta. Pour mixture into a lightly greased 11x7-inch baking dish. Sprinkle Cheddar cheese on top. Bake 10 minutes. Serves 6.

 Make It Modern: Substitute 3–4 fresh tomatoes, diced, for canned tomatoes.

Rancheros Casserole

INGREDIENTS

- 1 **pound ground beef**
- 2 **(4.5-ounce) packages au gratin potatoes**
- 3⅔ **cups boiling water**
- 1 **(15-ounce) can whole-kernel corn, drained**
- 1 **cup milk**
- 8 **ounces shredded taco-seasoned cheese, divided**

Preheat oven to 400°F.

Cook beef in a skillet over medium heat until beef is no longer pink; drain. Mix together potatoes and sauce mix from package, 3⅔ cups boiling water, corn, and milk in a large bowl. Stir in beef mixture and ½ cheese. Pour mixture into a lightly greased 2-quart casserole dish. Bake, uncovered, 30–35 minutes. Top with remaining ½ cheese. Let cheese melt and casserole set for 10 minutes before serving. Serves 6.

Sam's Tamale Pie

INGREDIENTS

- 1 **pound ground beef, lightly seasoned with salt**
- ½ **pound bulk pork sausage**
- 1 **tablespoon corn oil**
- 1 **cup chopped onion**
- 2 **cloves garlic, finely chopped**
- 1 **(28-ounce) can tomatoes, cut up**
- 1 **(10-ounce) package frozen corn**
- 1½ **cups shredded Cheddar cheese, divided**
- 1 **tablespoon chili powder**
- ¾ **teaspoon ground cumin**
- ½ **cup sliced black olives**
- 2 **tablespoons canned diced green chilies**
- 1 **cup whole milk**
- 2 **eggs, lightly beaten**
- 1 **cup cornmeal, plus pinch salt**

Preheat oven to 375°F.

Cook beef and sausage in a large saucepan over medium heat until meat is no longer pink; drain and return to pan. Add oil; stir in onion and garlic, and cook 2 minutes. Add tomatoes, corn, ½ cup Cheddar cheese, chili powder, and cumin; stir well. Simmer 10 minutes; stir in olives and green chilies. Pour meat mixture into a lightly greased 13x9x2-inch glass baking dish. Mix together milk, eggs, and cornmeal in a bowl. Spoon milk mixture evenly over meat mixture in baking dish. Sprinkle with 1 cup Cheddar cheese. Bake, uncovered, 40–50 minutes or until golden brown. Serves 6.

Note: This cornbread-topped hot dish is meaty and a little spicy but not too hot. Like Sam, it's unforgettable.

Taco Hot Dish

INGREDIENTS

- 2 **pounds ground beef**
- 1 **cup chopped onion**
- 3 **cloves garlic, chopped**
- 1 **(15-ounce) can tomato sauce**
- 1 **(1¼-ounce) packet taco seasoning mix**
- 1 **(16-ounce) can kidney beans, undrained**
- 1 **(9.25-ounce) package corn chips**
- 2 **cups shredded Cheddar cheese**

Preheat oven to 350°F.

Cook beef, onion, and garlic in a saucepan over medium heat until beef is no longer pink; drain, reserving 1 tablespoon drippings, and return beef mixture to pan. Stir in tomato sauce and taco seasoning mix; simmer 25 minutes, stirring often. Stir in beans. Layer ½ beef mixture, ½ corn chips, and ½ cheese in a lightly greased, shallow 2½-quart baking dish. Repeat layers, ending with cheese. Bake 45 minutes. Serves 8.

Note: Tacos were hard to find in Minnesota in the early 1950s, but they're now a favorite food. Serve this taco-like hot dish with shredded lettuce, diced onion, chopped tomatoes, olives, and sour cream.

Taco-Style Lasagna

INGREDIENTS

- 1 **pound ground beef, turkey, or chicken**
- 1 **tablespoon instant minced onion**
- 1 **(15-ounce) can tomato sauce**
- 1 **(16-ounce) jar thick-and-chunky salsa**
- 12 **pieces oven-ready lasagna, uncooked**
- 4 **cups shredded sharp Cheddar cheese, divided**
- ¼ **cup crushed tortilla chips (optional)**
- ¼ **cup sliced ripe black olives (optional)**

Preheat oven to 375°F.

Cook beef and onion in a large saucepan over medium heat until beef is no longer pink; drain and return beef mixture to pan. Stir together tomato sauce and salsa in a bowl; spread ½ cup on bottom of a lightly greased 13x9x2-inch baking dish. Add remaining tomato sauce mixture to beef mixture in pan; bring meat sauce to a boil, and then simmer. Place 3 lasagna pieces crosswise in baking dish. Pasta should not overlap or touch sides of pan (pasta will expand when baked). Spread ⅔ cup meat sauce over pasta, covering pasta completely. Sprinkle evenly with 1 cup cheese. Repeat layers twice, and top with remaining 3 pasta pieces. Spread remaining meat sauce on top, covering pasta completely; sprinkle with remaining 1 cup cheese. Cover with aluminum foil. Bake 35 minutes or until hot and bubbly. Let stand 10 minutes before cutting. Sprinkle with tortilla chips and olives, if desired. Serves 8–10.

Note: Serve with a crisp green salad and your favorite bread.

Beef 'n' Barley Hot Dish

INGREDIENTS

- 1 pound ground beef
- 1 tablespoon corn oil
- 1 medium-size onion, chopped
- 2 cloves garlic, chopped
- 1 cup uncooked barley
- ½ cup diced celery
- 1 (14.5-ounce) can whole tomatoes, cut up and undrained
- 2½ cups water
- 2 teaspoons salt
- Pinch ground black pepper

Preheat oven to 350°F.

Cook beef in a skillet over medium heat until no longer pink; drain, reserving 1 tablespoon drippings in skillet. Place beef in a lightly greased 2½-quart baking dish. Add corn oil, onion, garlic, and barley to skillet; cook while stirring until onion is browned. Add celery and next 4 ingredients; mix well and stir into beef mixture in baking dish. Cover and bake 2 hours. Serves 6.

Note: This hot dish is a bit like a beef-barley soup that Theresa liked to make. Serve this hot dish with buttered carrots and a broccoli salad.

Beef Pot Pie

INGREDIENTS

- 2 **prepared piecrusts, divided**
- 2 **cups diced, cooked potatoes**
- 1 **(10-ounce) package frozen mixed vegetables, thawed**
- 1½ **cups diced, cooked roast beef**
- 1 **(10½-ounce) can condensed cream of mushroom soup, undiluted**
- ⅓ **cup water**
- 1 **teaspoon Worcestershire sauce**
- ¾ **teaspoon crushed thyme leaves**

Preheat oven to 350°F.

Place 1 piecrust in a 9-inch deep-dish pie plate. Arrange potatoes, vegetables, and beef in piecrust. Mix together soup, water, Worcestershire sauce, and thyme in a bowl; pour soup mixture over beef. Top with remaining piecrust. Seal edges of crust. Cut slits in top to let out steam. Bake 35 minutes or until crust is golden brown. Serves 4.

Beef Stroganoff

INGREDIENTS

- 3 tablespoons butter
- 2 pounds sirloin steak, thinly sliced into 1-inch diagonal strips and lightly seasoned with salt and ground black pepper
- 1 large onion, thinly sliced
- 1 pound fresh mushrooms, sliced
- 3 tablespoons all-purpose flour
- 1½ cups beef broth
- ½ cup dry red wine or apple juice
- 2 teaspoons paprika
- ¼ teaspoon dried dill weed
- Pinch ground nutmeg
- 3 cloves garlic, minced
- 1 cup sour cream
- Cooked buttered noodles
- Minced parsley

Preheat oven to 350°F.

Melt butter in a large saucepan. Add beef; cook while stirring until no longer pink. Remove beef to a lightly greased 3-quart glass baking dish. Cook onion and mushrooms in drippings in saucepan until tender. Stir in flour until blended. Stir in broth and next 5 ingredients. Quickly bring to a boil. Remove from heat; pour broth mixture over beef in baking dish. Cover and bake 1½ hours or until meat is very tender. Gradually stir in sour cream. Serve over cooked noodles; sprinkle with parsley. Serves 6.

Note: This hot dish is a classic. You can use other cuts of beef for stroganoff, if desired.

Cajun John's Jambalaya

INGREDIENTS

- 1¼ cups long-grain white rice, uncooked
- 2 tablespoons corn oil
- 1 cup chopped onion
- 1 large green bell pepper, chopped
- 3 cloves garlic, chopped
- 2 stalks celery, chopped
- ¾ pound smoked beef sausage, sliced into ½-inch pieces
- 1 pound uncooked, medium-size peeled fresh shrimp, cut in half crosswise
- 2 (14.5-ounce) cans stewed tomatoes, chopped and undrained
- ½ teaspoon salt
- ¼ teaspoon cayenne pepper
- 1½ cups water or chicken stock

Preheat oven to 350°F.

Spread rice evenly on bottom of a lightly greased 3½-quart glass baking dish. Heat oil in a large saucepan over medium-high heat. Add onion and bell pepper; cook while stirring 1 minute. Add garlic and celery; cook while stirring a few seconds. Remove vegetables to a large bowl. Add sausage to saucepan, and cook while stirring 3 minutes; drain, reserving 1 tablespoon drippings in pan. Cook shrimp in drippings in saucepan until pink. Combine sausage, shrimp, and next 3 ingredients with vegetables in large bowl. Spoon sausage mixture evenly over rice. Pour 1½ cups water over top. Cover tightly; bake 1 hour or until rice is tender. Serves 6.

Note: Jambalaya means "mixture." You can add cubed cooked chicken and pork to this dish, if desired. A crisp tossed salad and fresh French bread complete this Cajun meal.

Cheddar Burger Skillet

INGREDIENTS

- 1 **pound ground beef**
- 1 **medium-size onion, chopped**
- 1 **(10½-ounce) can condensed cream of mushroom soup, undiluted**
- 1 **(10¾-ounce) can Cheddar cheese soup**
- ¼ **cup water**
- 2 **(14.5-ounce) cans whole potatoes, drained and sliced**
- 1 **(14.5-ounce) can French-cut green beans, drained**

Preheat oven to 350°F.

Cook beef and onion in a large skillet over medium heat until beef is no longer pink; drain and return to skillet. Stir in soups and ¼ cup water. Add potatoes and green beans. Place beef mixture into a lightly greased 11x7-inch baking dish, and bake 30 minutes. Serves 6.

Make It Modern: Substitute fresh potatoes for canned potatoes. Boil 3–4 peeled and quartered potatoes 12–14 minutes; cool and cut into slices.

New Shepherd's Pie

INGREDIENTS

- 1 tablespoon corn oil
- 1 medium-size onion, chopped
- 1 pound lean ground beef
- 2 cloves garlic, chopped
- 1 (12-ounce) jar home-style beef gravy or homemade beef gravy
- 2 tablespoons ketchup
- ½ (16-ounce) package frozen mixed vegetables
- 2 cups water
- 2 tablespoons butter
- ¼ teaspoon salt
- 2½ cups instant mashed potato flakes or equal amount homemade
- 1 cup whole milk
- 1 egg, lightly beaten
- ½ cup shredded Cheddar cheese
- Paprika

Preheat oven to 375°F.

Heat oil in a large saucepan over medium heat. Add onion and beef; cook until beef is no longer pink; drain, and return beef mixture to pan. Stir in garlic, gravy, ketchup, and vegetables. Bring to a boil; reduce heat, and simmer 8 minutes. Place beef mixture into a lightly greased 2-quart glass baking dish. Bring 2 cups water to a boil in a saucepan. Add butter and salt; stir. Remove from heat. Stir in potato flakes and milk. Let rest 5 minutes. Add egg to potatoes; mix well. Add cheese; mix well. Spread potato mixture evenly over top of beef mixture. Sprinkle lightly with paprika. Bake 25 minutes or until potatoes are set and lightly browned. Serves 4.

Note: The original shepherd's pie was made with a thin lining of mashed potatoes on the bottom of the dish, filled with cubed cooked lamb and lamb gravy, then topped with more mashed potatoes.

Potato-Carrot Hot Dish

INGREDIENTS

- 1 **pound ground beef**
- 1 **medium-size onion, diced**
- 1 **cup celery**
- 3 **medium-size carrots, peeled and diced**
- 3 **medium-size potatoes, peeled and diced**
- ¼ **cup Minute Rice, uncooked**
- 1 **(10½-ounce) can condensed cream of mushroom soup, undiluted**
- 1 **(10½-ounce) can condensed cream of chicken soup, undiluted**
- 1 **cup milk**
- **Salt and pepper**

Preheat oven to 350°F.

Cook beef with onion and celery in a skillet over medium heat until beef is no longer pink; drain. Cook carrots and potatoes in water to cover in a saucepan 10 minutes; drain. Combine beef mixture, carrots and potatoes, rice, and next 4 ingredients in a lightly greased 11x7-inch baking dish. Bake 1–1½ hours. Serves 6.

Swedish Meatballs

INGREDIENTS

- 4 tablespoons butter, divided
- ½ cup minced onion
- 1¼ pounds ground beef
- ¼ pound ground pork
- ¼ teaspoon salt
- ¼ teaspoon ground black pepper
- Pinch ground nutmeg
- 1 cup unseasoned breadcrumbs
- ½ cup whole milk
- 1 egg, plus 1 yolk, lightly beaten
- 2 tablespoons all-purpose flour, mixed with ¼ teaspoon salt, ¼ teaspoon paprika, and pinch of ground black pepper
- 1¼ cups skim milk
- Hot cooked noodles, buttered

Preheat oven to 350°F.

Melt 2 tablespoons butter in a large saucepan over medium heat; add onion. Cook while stirring until onion is soft but not brown; spoon onion mixture into a large bowl. Add beef and next 7 ingredients to bowl. Mix gently, and form beef mixture into 1-inch meatballs; place in pan, and brown on all sides. Place browned meatballs into a lightly greased 2½-quart glass baking dish. Melt remaining 2 tablespoons butter in pan over medium heat. Gradually add flour mixture, stirring constantly until blended. Gradually stir in skim milk; cook while stirring until thickened. Pour milk mixture over meatballs in baking dish. Cover and bake 50 minutes. Serve over buttered hot cooked noodles. Serves 6.

Note: Swedish Meatballs are very popular in Minnesota, as there are many blonde Swedes living here! Serve this hot dish with buttered peas and your favorite bread.

Tater Tot Hot Dish

INGREDIENTS

- 1 pound ground beef, lightly seasoned with ground black pepper
- ½ cup chopped onion (optional)
- 1 (10½-ounce) can condensed cream of chicken soup, undiluted
- 1 cup canned green beans, peas, or creamed corn

Frozen Tater Tots

- 1 (10½-ounce) can condensed cream of mushroom soup, undiluted

Preheat oven to 350°F.

Spread uncooked beef onto bottom of a lightly greased 9x9-inch baking dish. Sprinkle evenly with onion, if desired. Top with cream of chicken soup, then green beans. Spread with enough frozen Tater Tots to cover top. Pour cream of mushroom soup over all. Bake 55 minutes. Serves 4.

Note: This hot dish was a hit when frozen Tater Tots came out years ago, and its popularity is still going. Serve it with crusty rolls.

Pork

Effie's Chili Hot Dish

INGREDIENTS

- ½ **pound bulk pork sausage**
- ½ **pound ground beef**
- 1 **cup chopped onion**
- 2 **tablespoons chopped green bell pepper**
- 3 **cloves garlic, chopped**
- ½ **teaspoon salt**
- ¼ **teaspoon ground black pepper**
- 1 **(8-ounce) can tomato sauce**
- 1 **(14.5-ounce) can whole tomatoes, cut up and undrained**
- 2 **(16-ounce) cans pinto beans, drained**
- 2 **teaspoons chili powder**
- **Pinch cayenne pepper**
- 2 **teaspoons brown sugar**
- 1 **tablespoon white vinegar**
- 2 **teaspoons prepared mustard**

Preheat oven to 375°F.

Cook pork sausage, ground beef, onion, bell pepper, garlic, salt, and pepper in a large saucepan over medium heat until sausage and beef are no longer pink; drain and return sausage mixture to pan. Stir in tomato sauce and tomatoes; cook while stirring 2 minutes. Stir in pinto beans and next 5 ingredients; mix well. Pour mixture into a lightly greased 2½-quart baking dish. Bake, uncovered, 45 minutes. Serves 6.

Note: Serve this hot dish with a crisp salad and warm corn muffins—buttered, of course.

Sausage Chili Hot Dish

INGREDIENTS

- 1 **tablespoon olive oil**
- 1 **cup chopped onion**
- 2 **cloves garlic, coarsely chopped**
- ¾ **cup chopped green bell pepper**
- 1 **pound Italian sausage, crumbled**
- 1 **cup long-grain white rice, uncooked**
- 1 **(16-ounce) can kidney beans, drained**
- 1 **(14.5-ounce) can diced tomatoes with jalapeños and spices, undrained**
- 2 **cups chicken broth**
- ½ **cup water**
- 2 **teaspoons chili powder**
- ¼ **teaspoon ground cumin**
- 1 **cup shredded Cheddar cheese**

Preheat oven to 375°F.

Heat oil in a large saucepan over medium heat. Add onion, garlic, and bell pepper; cook while stirring 1 minute. Add sausage, and cook until sausage is no longer pink. Drain, reserving 1 tablespoon drippings in pan, and remove sausage mixture to a large bowl. Add rice to drippings in saucepan; cook while stirring 3 minutes. Add rice, beans, and next 5 ingredients to bowl with sausage mixture. Mix well. Spoon mixture into a lightly greased 13x9x2-inch glass baking dish. Cover with aluminum foil. Bake 1 hour. Remove foil; top with cheese. Bake, uncovered, until cheese is melted. Serves 6–8.

Note: All you need with this chili hot dish is a green salad and freshly baked corn muffins.

Broccoli 'n' Ham Hot Dish

INGREDIENTS

- 1 (4-ounce) jar Cheez Whiz
- 1 (10½-ounce) can condensed cream of chicken soup, undiluted
- ½ cup whole milk
- 2 tablespoons butter
- ½ cup chopped onion
- 1 (10-ounce) package frozen chopped broccoli
- 2 cups diced fully cooked ham
- 1 cup Minute Rice, uncooked
- ¼ teaspoon Worcestershire sauce

Preheat oven to 350°F.

Blend cheese, soup, and milk in a large bowl. Melt butter in a saucepan over medium heat; cook onion while stirring until tender. Add onion to cheese mixture in bowl. Cook broccoli according to package directions un,til just tender but not done; drain and add to bowl. Stir in ham, rice, and Worcestershire sauce; mix well. Spoon mixture into 2 lightly greased 1½-quart glass baking dishes. Cover tightly. Bake 1 hour. Serves 6.

Note: This hot dish freezes well. If frozen, bake, uncovered, 1½ hours.

Ham and Broccoli Bake

INGREDIENTS

- 1 (4.7-ounce) package au gratin potatoes
- 3 cups boiling water
- 1 teaspoon salt
- 3 tablespoons margarine, divided
- 3 eggs, lightly beaten and divided
- 1½ cups diced cooked ham
- 1 (10-ounce) package chopped broccoli, thawed and drained
- 1½ cups shredded Swiss cheese, divided
- ½ cup milk
- ¼ teaspoon prepared mustard

Preheat oven to 375°F.

Place potatoes in a large saucepan (reserve sauce packet), and cover with 3 cups boiling water; add salt, and let stand 15 minutes. Drain off water, and stir in 1 tablespoon margarine and 1 egg. Press potato mixture in bottom and up sides of a lightly greased 10-inch square baking dish. Bake 10 minutes. Meanwhile, combine ham, broccoli, ½ cup cheese, and remaining 2 eggs in a large bowl. Heat remaining 2 tablespoons margarine in a saucepan. Add sauce packet from au gratin potatoes, milk, and mustard; bring to a boil and stir 1 minute. Stir sauce mixture into ham mixture in bowl. Spoon mixture into prepared potato shell. Bake 30 minutes; sprinkle remaining 1 cup cheese on top. Bake until cheese is melted. Remove from oven, and let stand 5 minutes before serving. Serves 4.

Ham 'n' Corn Hot Dish

INGREDIENTS

- 1 **cup cubed cooked ham**
- ½ **cup chopped onion**
- ½ **cup chopped red bell pepper**
- 1 **(14.75-ounce) can creamed corn**
- 1 **(10-ounce) package frozen whole-kernel corn, thawed**
- ½ **cup whole milk**
- 1 **(8-ounce) package seasoned bread cubes**
- 3 **tablespoons butter, melted**
- 1 **tablespoon Worcestershire sauce**
- 2 **tablespoons grated Parmesan cheese**

Preheat oven to 350°F.

Combine ham and next 5 ingredients in a bowl; mix well. Spoon ham mixture into a buttered 2-quart glass baking dish. Top with bread cubes. Combine melted butter and Worcestershire sauce in a small bowl; spoon evenly over bread cubes. Bake, uncovered, 40 minutes. Top with Parmesan cheese, and bake until melted. Serves 4.

Note: Serve this hot dish with a crisp green salad.

Hue's Ham-Corn Hot Dish

INGREDIENTS

- 3 tablespoons butter
- 3 tablespoons all-purpose flour
- 1½ cups whole milk
- ¾ teaspoon dry mustard
- ¼ teaspoon ground black pepper
- ½ teaspoon Worcestershire sauce
- ½ cup finely chopped onion
- ½ cup finely diced green bell pepper
- 1 (15-ounce) can whole-kernel corn
- 2 cups diced cooked ham
- ½ cup shredded sharp Cheddar cheese
- ¼ cup plain dry breadcrumbs, mixed with 1 tablespoon melted butter

Preheat oven to 350°F.

Melt butter in a large saucepan over medium heat. Gradually stir in flour. Gradually stir in milk; cook while stirring until smooth. Stir in dry mustard and next 7 ingredients; mix well. Spoon mixture into a lightly greased 2-quart baking dish. Top with breadcrumbs. Bake, uncovered, 40 minutes. Serves 6.

Note: Serve this tasty hot dish with a lettuce, tomato, and cucumber salad, along with warm crusty bread.

Cheese and Sausage Pasta Bake

INGREDIENTS

- 1 **pound pasta**
- 1 **pound Polska Kielbasa or smoked sausage**
- 1 **(24-ounce) jar spaghetti sauce**
- 2 **cups cottage cheese**
- 2 **cups shredded mozzarella cheese, divided**
- ¼ **cup Parmesan cheese**

Preheat oven to 350°F.

Cook pasta according to package directions; drain. Slice sausage into ½-inch pieces, and cook in a large skillet over medium heat until lightly browned. Stir in pasta and spaghetti sauce. Gently stir in cottage cheese and 1 cup mozzarella cheese. Pour pasta mixture into a lightly greased 11x7-inch baking dish. Top with remaining 1 cup mozzarella cheese and Parmesan cheese. Bake 30 minutes. Serves 4–6.

Ham 'n' Noodles Hot Dish

INGREDIENTS

8 ounces spaghetti noodles, cooked according to package directions and drained

2 cups cubed cooked ham

2 cups shredded Swiss cheese

1 (10½-ounce) can condensed cream of celery soup, undiluted

1 cup sour cream

½ cup chopped onion

½ cup chopped green bell pepper

Preheat oven to 350°F.

Combine spaghetti noodles, ham, and cheese in a large bowl. Combine soup, sour cream, onion, and green pepper in a small bowl. Layer ⅓ noodle mixture and ½ soup mixture in a lightly greased 13x9x2-inch baking dish. Repeat layers, and top with remaining ⅓ noodle mixture. Bake, uncovered, 45 minutes or until very hot. Serves 6.

Note: A green salad and rolls completes this meal.

Macaroni Ham and Cheese

INGREDIENTS

- 1¼ cups elbow macaroni, uncooked
- 5 tablespoons butter
- ½ cup chopped onion
- ¼ cup chopped green bell pepper
- 5 tablespoons all-purpose flour
- ½ teaspoon salt
- ¼ teaspoon black pepper
- 2 cups whole milk
- 8 ounces American or Swiss cheese, cut up
- 1¼ cups cubed or diced cooked ham

Preheat oven to 375°F.

Cook macaroni in salted water until just barely tender; drain and place in a lightly greased 1½-quart glass baking dish. Melt butter in a heavy saucepan over medium heat. Add onion and green bell pepper; cook while stirring until just tender but not brown. Gradually stir in flour; cook while stirring until well blended. Add salt and pepper. Stir in milk. Bring to a boil, stirring constantly; boil 1 minute. Stir in cheese until melted. Stir in ham. Pour ham mixture over macaroni in baking dish; stir well. Bake, uncovered, 35 minutes. Serves 6.

Note: Serve with fresh sliced tomatoes and hard rolls.

Sausage with Rigatoni

INGREDIENTS

- **4 cups broccoli florets**
- **1¼ pounds hot Italian sausage, casings removed**
- **½ cup finely chopped onion**
- **1 (26-ounce) jar marinara sauce**
- **1 (8-ounce) package shredded part-skim mozzarella cheese**
- **2 tablespoons freshly grated Parmesan cheese**
- **1 pound rigatoni, cooked according to package directions**

Preheat oven to 375°F.

Pour water to 1 inch deep in a 4-quart saucepan; bring to a boil. Add broccoli. Reduce heat to low; cover and simmer 2 minutes, and drain. Break up sausage with a spoon in a large skillet. Add onion; cook and stir until sausage is well browned. Add marinara sauce; stir until heated through. Combine broccoli, sausage mixture, cheeses, and rigatoni in a large bowl. Spoon mixture into a lightly greased, shallow 2½-quart baking dish. Cover with aluminum foil. Bake 25 minutes or until bubbly and cheese is melted. Serves 6.

Note: Theresa liked to make her own marinara sauce, but the jarred sauce is so handy. Serve this hot dish with a green salad.

Cheesy Potatoes with Smoked Sausage

INGREDIENTS

- 1 (14-ounce) package smoked sausage
- 1 (20-ounce) package refrigerated, shredded hash brown potatoes
- 2 cups shredded Cheddar cheese
- 1 cup sour cream
- ¼ cup margarine, melted
- 1 cup precooked broccoli and carrots

Preheat oven to 350°F.

Cut sausage into ½-inch cubes. Combine sausage, potatoes, and next 4 ingredients in a large bowl. Spread sausage mixture evenly into a lightly greased 9x13-inch baking dish. Bake 45–50 minutes or until lightly browned. Let stand 5 minutes before serving. Serves 4.

Country Sausage Casserole

INGREDIENTS

- 1 pound Polska Kielbasa, cut into ½-inch slices
- 1 tablespoon vegetable oil
- 1 (4.7-ounce) package au gratin potatoes
- 2 cups hot water
- ½ cup milk
- 2 cups chopped broccoli
- 2 cups carrots, diced
- 1 cup canned corn, drained
- 1 cup shredded Cheddar cheese

Preheat oven to 350˚F.

Cook sausage in oil in a large saucepan over medium heat until browned. Stir in au gratin potatoes and sauce mix, 2 cups hot water, and milk; bring sausage mixture to a boil. Reduce heat, cover, and simmer 10 minutes. Meanwhile, cook broccoli and carrots in a saucepan over medium heat until tender. Add broccoli-carrot mixture to sausage mixture; stir in corn, and mix well. Pour mixture into a lightly greased 11x7-inch baking dish. Bake 25 minutes. Top with cheese, and bake 5 minutes. Serves 6.

 Make It Modern: Try a pound of a different kind of sausage, such as brats, instead of Polska Kielbasa.

Ham and Potatoes Au Gratin

INGREDIENTS

- **4 medium-size potatoes, thinly sliced**
- **1½ cups diced cooked ham**
- **1 (10¾-ounce) can Cheddar cheese soup, undiluted**
- **½ cup milk**
- **½ cup sour cream**
- **1 cup green beans or corn**

Preheat oven to 350°F.

Combine potatoes and ham in a large bowl. Cook soup, milk, sour cream, and green beans in a saucepan over medium heat just until heated. Stir soup mixture into potato mixture. Pour mixture into a lightly greased 11x7-inch casserole dish. Cover and bake 1½ hours or until potatoes are tender. Serves 6.

Ham-Potatoes Hot Dish

INGREDIENTS

1 **tablespoon butter**

¼ **cup chopped green onion**

¼ **cup chopped green bell pepper**

4 **medium-size russet potatoes, thinly sliced into rounds**

1½ **cups cubed cooked ham**

1 **(10¾-ounce) can Cheddar cheese soup, undiluted**

½ **cup sour cream**

½ **cup whole milk**

¼ **cup shredded Cheddar cheese**

Pinch ground black pepper

1 **cup frozen peas and carrots, thawed**

Preheat oven to 350°F.

Melt butter in a saucepan over medium heat. Add onion and green bell pepper. Cook while stirring until soft; spoon onion mixture into a large bowl. Add potatoes and ham to onion mixture in bowl. Heat soup, sour cream, milk, cheese, and black pepper in saucepan over medium heat; stir until cheese is melted. Add peas and carrots to pan; cook while stirring until bubbly. Pour soup mixture over potato mixture in bowl; mix well. Spoon mixture into a lightly greased 2-quart glass baking dish. Cover tightly. Bake 1½–2 hours or until potatoes are done. Serves 4–6.

Note: Simple and quick to prepare, this hot dish goes great with sliced tomatoes, a crisp green salad, and warm rolls.

Potato-Sausage Bake

INGREDIENTS

- 2 **tablespoons vegetable oil**
- 6 **cups diced, cooked potatoes (4 large potatoes)**
- 1 **(12-ounce) package Hormel Little Sizzlers, cooked according to package directions and diced**
- 6 **eggs, lightly beaten**
- ½ **cup mozzarella cheese**
- ½ **cup Cheddar cheese**

Preheat oven to 350°F.

Heat oil in a large skillet over medium heat. Add potatoes and cook until slightly browned. Stir in sausage. Pour eggs while whisking them over potatoes and sausage; cook, stirring occasionally, until eggs are done. Place mixture into a lightly greased 9x13-inch pan. Top with cheeses, and bake 10–15 minutes or until cheese is melted. Serves 4–6.

 Make It Modern: Substitute Jimmy Dean sage sausage for Little Sizzlers.

Scalloped Potatoes and Ham

INGREDIENTS

5 tablespoons butter, divided

¼ cup all-purpose flour

3 cups whole milk

1 teaspoon dried parsley flakes

1 teaspoon salt

½ teaspoon dried thyme

¼ teaspoon ground black pepper

6 cups thinly sliced peeled potatoes

1½ cups chopped cooked ham

1 small onion, grated

Preheat oven to 375°F.

Melt 4 tablespoons butter in a saucepan over medium heat. Stir in flour; gradually stir in milk. Stir in parsley, salt, thyme, and pepper. Bring sauce mixture to a boil; cook while stirring 2 minutes. Combine potatoes and next 2 ingredients in a large bowl; spoon ½ potato mixture into a lightly greased 2½-quart baking dish. Top with ½ sauce mixture. Repeat layers. Cover and bake 1 hour and 10 minutes or until potatoes are almost done. Uncover; dot with remaining 1 tablespoon butter. Bake, uncovered, 15 minutes or until potatoes are done. Serves 6.

Note: This is an old favorite hot dish that's always tasty. Serve it with a crisp green salad and sliced fresh tomatoes.

Spuds and Chops Hot Dish

INGREDIENTS

- 4 thick pork chops, seasoned lightly with salt and pepper
- 1 tablespoon corn oil
- 4 medium-size potatoes, peeled and quartered, boiled in lightly salted water until just tender, and drained
- 1½ tablespoons butter
- 1 large onion, cut into rings
- 1½ tablespoons all-purpose flour
- 1 cup chicken or beef bouillon
- 1½ teaspoons vinegar
- ¼ teaspoon garlic salt
- Salt and black pepper
- 1 cup sour cream

Preheat oven to 375°F.

Brown pork chops in oil in a saucepan over medium heat. Place chops into a lightly greased shallow 2-quart glass baking dish. Spoon potatoes over chops. Melt butter in saucepan over medium heat. Add onion; cook while stirring until soft. Spoon onion slices over potatoes, reserving butter in pan. Gradually add flour to butter in pan; cook while stirring 2 minutes but do not brown. Stir in bouillon, vinegar, and garlic salt. Add salt and pepper to taste. Remove sauce mixture from heat. Stir in sour cream until blended. Pour mixture over all. Cover; bake 35 minutes. Uncover and bake 30 minutes. Serves 4.

Note: Here's a good hot dish for that special "meat and potatoes" person in your life.

Italian Sausage-Rice Hot Dish

INGREDIENTS

- 1 pound Italian sausage, casings removed
- ½ cup chopped onion
- 1½ cups tender zucchini, cut into ¼-inch slices
- 3 cloves garlic, minced
- 1 (13.8-ounce) package chicken-flavor rice and pasta mix, prepared according to package directions
- 2½ cups spaghetti sauce, divided
- ½ teaspoon dried basil
- 1 cups shredded mozzarella cheese, divided

Preheat oven to 350°F.

Crumble sausage into a large skillet over medium heat. Add onion, and cook while stirring until sausage is browned; drain, reserving 1 tablespoon drippings in skillet. Remove sausage mixture to a large bowl. Add zucchini and garlic to drippings in skillet; cook while stirring over medium-high heat 1 minute. Cover and cook 2 minutes. Stir rice, 1½ cups spaghetti sauce, and basil into sausage mixture in bowl. Spoon rice mixture into a lightly greased 2½-quart baking dish. Sprinkle with 1 cup cheese. Top with zucchini mixture. Top with remaining 1 cup spaghetti sauce; sprinkle with remaining 1 cup cheese. Bake 30 minutes or until thoroughly heated. Serves 8.

Note: Serve with a green salad tossed with Italian dressing and Parmesan cheese.

Pork Chops Hot Dish

INGREDIENTS

- 4 (1-inch-thick) pork chops
- 2 tablespoons corn oil
- 1¼ cups long-grain white rice, uncooked
- 1 (14.5-ounce) can diced tomatoes
- 1 (10½-ounce) can condensed beef consommé, undiluted
- 1 (2-ounce) package dry onion soup mix
- ½ teaspoon thyme
- ½ teaspoon oregano
- ½ teaspoon salt
- Pinch ground black pepper

Preheat oven to 350°F.

Brown pork chops in oil in a heavy saucepan over medium heat. Place rice in a lightly greased, shallow 2-quart glass baking dish. Place pork chops on top of rice. Combine tomatoes and next 6 ingredients in saucepan; mix well. Pour tomato mixture over chops. Cover and bake 1¼ hours. Serves 4.

Note: A broccoli slaw goes well with this pork chop hot dish. Serve with chunky applesauce.

Sausage-Wild Rice Hot Dish

INGREDIENTS

- 1 cup long-grain and wild rice, uncooked
- 1 pound bulk sausage
- 1 (4-ounce) can sliced mushrooms, drained
- 1 (10½-ounce) can condensed cream of mushroom soup, undiluted
- 1 medium-size onion, thinly sliced

Preheat oven to 350°F.

Cook rice, according to package directions, in a saucepan until tender but not mushy; drain. Cook sausage in a large saucepan over medium heat until sausage is no longer pink; drain and return to pan. Stir in mushrooms and soup. Stir in rice; mix well. Spoon ½ mixture into a buttered 2-quart glass baking dish. Top with onion. Spoon remaining ½ mixture evenly over onion. Bake, covered, 1 hour. Serves 4.

Note: This is a good hot dish to add to a brunch selection.

Wild Rice and Ham Pie

INGREDIENTS

- 1 readymade piecrust
- 1 teaspoon all-purpose flour
- 1 cup diced cooked ham
- ½ cup cooked long-grain and wild rice
- ⅓ cup chopped red bell pepper
- ¼ cup chopped green onion tops
- 1 (4.5-ounce) jar sliced mushrooms, drained
- 3 eggs, lighty beaten
- 1 cup sour cream
- 1 tablespoon prepared mustard
- ½ teaspoon salt
- Dash ground black pepper
- 2 cups shredded Swiss cheese, divided

Preheat oven to 425°F.

Place piecrust into a 9-inch pie plate. Do not prick crust. Bake 10–12 minutes or until golden brown. Remove from oven and reduce heat to 400°F. Combine flour and next 5 ingredients in a large bowl. Combine eggs, sour cream, mustard, salt, and pepper in a small bowl; blend well. Sprinkle 1 cup cheese into baked crust. Spread ham mixture over cheese. Pour egg mixture over top. Top with remaining 1 cup cheese. Bake 30–35 minutes until filling is set. Cool 10 minutes. Serves 4.

Zucchini-Sausage-Rice Hot Dish

INGREDIENTS

- 1 **pound Italian sausage, casings removed**
- ½ **cup chopped onion**
- 2 **small zucchini, cut into ¼-inch slices**
- 2 **cloves garlic, minced**
- 1 **(13.8-ounce) package chicken-flavor rice-and-pasta mix, prepared according to package directions**
- ½ **teaspoon dried basil**
- 2 **cups shredded mozzarella cheese, divided**

Preheat oven to 350°F.

Crumble sausage into a large saucepan over medium heat. Add onion; cook while stirring until sausage is browned. Drain, reserving 1 tablespoon drippings in saucepan, and remove sausage mixture to a large bowl. Stir zucchini and garlic into drippings in pan; cook while stirring over medium-high heat 1 minute. Cover and simmer 2 minutes. Add rice, and dried basil to sausage mixture in bowl; spoon sausage-rice mixture into a lightly greased 2½-quart glass baking dish. Top with zucchini mixture and cheese. Bake 30 minutes or until thoroughly heated. Serves 8.

Note: Serve with a green salad tossed with Italian dressing and grated Parmesan cheese.

Pork 'n' Beef Hot Dish

INGREDIENTS

- 1 (14.5-ounce) can diced tomatoes, undrained
- 1 cup water
- 3 tablespoons quick-cooking tapioca
- 1 teaspoon granulated sugar
- 1¼ teaspoons salt
- ¼ teaspoon ground black pepper
- 1 tablespoon corn oil
- 1½ pounds beef stew meat, cut into bite-size pieces
- ½ pound pork, cut into bite-size pieces
- 3 medium-size russet potatoes, peeled and quartered
- 3 carrots, peeled and cut into chunks
- 2 stalks celery, cut into chunks
- 1 large onion, cut into chunks
- 3 cloves garlic, chopped
- 1 tablespoon dry breadcrumbs

Preheat oven to 375°F.

Combine tomatoes, 1 cup water, tapioca, sugar, salt, and pepper in a large bowl. Heat oil in a saucepan over medium heat. Add beef and pork; cook while stirring until browned. Add meat to tomato mixture in bowl. Stir potatoes and next 5 ingredients into bowl; mix well. Pour mixture into a lightly greased 13x9x2-inch glass baking dish. Cover and bake 2 hours or until meat is tender. Serves 6.

Note: This hot dish is like a stew. Serve it in bowls along with crusty bread, or spoon it over hot cooked white rice and serve with a tossed green salad.

Spam Hot Dish

INGREDIENTS

- 1 (12-ounce) can Spam luncheon meat
- ½ pound cheese, grated
- ¾ cup cracker crumbs
- 1 (10½-ounce) can condensed cream of mushroom soup, undiluted
- 1 cup whole milk
- 3 eggs, lightly beaten
- 1 small onion, minced
- 1 small green bell pepper, minced

Preheat oven to 350°F.

Combine all ingredients in a large bowl; mix well. Pour mixture into a lightly greased 2-quart baking dish. Bake 1 hour. Serves 4–6.

Note: Spam originated in Minnesota. When it came on the store shelves, many dishes were created. This hot dish recipe dates back to the early 1950s.

Seafood

Broccoli and Crab Casserole

INGREDIENTS

- 1 (10-ounce) box frozen broccoli florets, thawed and cooked
- 1 (6-ounce) can crabmeat, drained
- ½ cup mayonnaise
- ¾ cup shredded Cheddar cheese

Preheat oven to 350°F.

Arrange cooked broccoli in a lightly greased 8-inch pan. Top with crabmeat. Spread mayonnaise over crabmeat, and top with cheese. Bake 30 minutes. Serves 4.

 Make It Modern: Substitute 1 bunch freshly steamed broccoli florets for frozen broccoli.

Tuna-Broccoli Hot Dish

INGREDIENTS

- 3 (5-ounce) cans tuna, drained and flaked
- 1½ cups cooked long-grain white rice
- 1 (10-ounce) package frozen chopped broccoli, cooked and drained
- ½ cup chopped onion
- 2 tablespoons chopped pimientos
- ½ teaspoon salt
- Pinch ground black pepper
- 1 (8-ounce) package cream cheese, cubed
- ¼ cup whole milk
- ¼ cup grated Parmesan cheese
- Garnish: fresh parsley sprigs

Preheat oven to 350°F.

Combine tuna, rice, broccoli, onion, pimientos, salt, and pepper in a large bowl. Heat cream cheese and milk in a saucepan over low heat, stirring until smooth. Stir in Parmesan cheese. Add cheese mixture to tuna mixture in bowl. Mix well. Spoon mixture into a lightly greased 10x6-inch baking dish. Bake 40 minutes. Garnish, if desired. Serves 6–8.

Note: Cream cheese makes this tuna hot dish special.

Crab Casserole

INGREDIENTS

1 (6-ounce) can crabmeat, drained

1 (10¾-ounce) can condensed cream of shrimp soup, mixed with ½ soup can of milk

½ cup mayonnaise

½ cup Cheddar cheese, grated

4 ounces egg noodles, uncooked

½ cup breadcrumbs

Preheat oven to 350°F.

Combine crabmeat and next 4 ingredients, and pour into a lightly greased 2-quart casserole dish. Cover and bake 40 minutes. Top evenly with breadcrumbs, and bake 5 minutes. Serves 4.

Doris's Tuna Hot Dish

INGREDIENTS

- 1½ cups whole milk
- 1 (8-ounce) package cream cheese, cut up
- 1 (10-ounce) package frozen peas, cooked and drained
- 7 ounces spaghetti noodles, cooked according to package directions and drained
- 2 (5-ounce) cans tuna, drained and flaked
- 1 (4-ounce) can mushrooms, drained
- ¼ cup grated Parmesan cheese
- 1 tablespoon chopped pimientos
- 1 tablespoon chopped onion
- ½ teaspoon onion salt
- ¼ teaspoon oregano leaves, crushed
- Pinch ground black pepper

Preheat oven to 350°F.

Heat milk and cream cheese in a large saucepan over low heat; stir until smooth. Add peas and next 9 ingredients; mix well. Pour mixture into a lightly greased 2-quart baking dish. Bake 25 minutes. Serves 6.

Note: Cousin Doris lives on a beautiful Minnesota lake, but she will often serve tuna as well as walleye!

 Make It Modern: Substitute fresh tuna, cooked, for canned tuna.

Favorite Tuna Hot Dish

INGREDIENTS

- 3½ cups elbow macaroni, cooked 3 minutes less than package directions and drained
- 2 (4.5-ounce) cans solid tuna, drained
- 1 (8.5-ounce) can small peas, drained
- 1 tablespoon minced onion
- 1¼ cups crushed potato chips, divided
- 1 (10½-ounce) can condensed cream of mushroom soup, undiluted
- 1½ cups whole milk

Preheat oven to 350°F.

Combine macaroni, tuna, peas, onion, and ½ cup potato chips in a buttered 2-quart glass baking dish. Bring soup and milk to a boil in a saucepan over medium heat, stirring constantly; pour soup mixture over macaroni mixture in baking dish. Top with remaining ¾ cup potato chips. Bake, uncovered, 35 minutes or until hot. Serves 4.

Note: Theresa's husband's Aunt Mollie served this tuna hot dish to her when she first came to Minnesota as a bride. Aunt Mollie served it with a molded lime gelatin salad. Theresa liked to serve it with a mixed green salad. Both options are good.

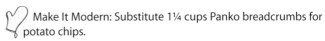 Make It Modern: Substitute 1¼ cups Panko breadcrumbs for potato chips.

Norse Fish Hot Dish

INGREDIENTS

- 3 tablespoons butter
- 3 tablespoons all-purpose flour, mixed with ¼ teaspoon salt and pinch ground black pepper
- 1¼ cups whole milk
- 2 eggs, separated
- 1 teaspoon ground nutmeg (optional)
- 1 pound cod fillets, cut into cubes
- 1 cup elbow macaroni, cooked a little less time than package directions
- 4 slices American cheese, cut into strips
- 5 tablespoons dry breadcrumbs
- 5 tablespoons melted butter, mixed with 2 teaspoons lemon juice and 2 tablespoons minced fresh parsley, kept warm

Preheat oven to 350°F.

Melt butter in a saucepan over medium heat. Stir in flour mixture. Stir in milk until smooth; cook while stirring over low heat until thickened, about 7 minutes. Beat egg yolks, and stir into milk mixture. Stir in nutmeg, if desired. In a large bowl, combine milk mixture, fish, and macaroni. In a small bowl, beat egg whites until stiff; fold into fish mixture. Pour mixture into a lightly greased 1½-quart baking dish. Top with cheese. Sprinkle with breadcrumbs. Bake 30 minutes. Top with warm butter mixture. Serves 4.

Note: Fish and Minnesota go together like cod and Norse!

Parmesan Shrimp Hot Dish

INGREDIENTS

- 6 tablespoons butter
- 3 cloves garlic, finely chopped
- 2 tablespoons minced onion
- 6 tablespoons all-purpose flour
- 2½ cups half-and-half
- ¾ cup clam juice
- 1 tablespoon ketchup
- ½ teaspoon salt
- ¼ teaspoon white pepper
- 1 tablespoon minced fresh dill
- ¾ cup Parmesan cheese, divided
- 1 (14-ounce) package farfalle (bow-tie) pasta, cooked according to package directions and drained
- 1 pound fresh shrimp, peeled and deveined

Preheat oven to 350°F.

Melt butter in a saucepan over medium heat. Add garlic and onion; cook while stirring 1 minute. Stir in flour to make a white roux (do not brown). Gradually stir in half-and-half. Add clam juice, ketchup, salt, pepper, dill, and 5 tablespoons Parmesan cheese; stir until sauce is well blended. Place pasta and shrimp into a lightly buttered 2-quart glass baking dish. Add sauce; stir to mix well. Sprinkle remaining 7 tablespoons Parmesan cheese on top. Bake, uncovered, 40 minutes or until bubbly. Serves 6.

Note: This is a good hot dish for company. Serve with French bread and a crisp green salad.

Salmon Casserole

INGREDIENTS

- 1 cup medium-size shell-shaped pasta, uncooked
- 2 (5-ounce) cans boneless, skinless salmon
- 2 tablespoons margarine
- 1 tablespoon all-purpose flour
- ¼ teaspoon salt
- 1 cup milk
- 2 teaspoons lemon juice
- 1 tablespoon chopped parsley
- 1 cup shredded Monterey Jack cheese, divided

Preheat oven to 375°F.

Cook pasta shells until tender; drain. Drain salmon, reserving liquid. Break salmon into small pieces. Melt margarine in a saucepan over medium heat. Stir in flour and salt. Add enough milk to reserved salmon liquid to make 1 cup. Gradually stir milk mixture into flour mixture in pan. Cook while stirring until mixture is thick and smooth. Add lemon juice and parsley. Combine pasta, salmon, milk mixture, and ¾ cup cheese. Pour mixture into a lightly greased 8-inch square baking dish. Top with remaining ¼ cup cheese. Bake 25 minutes. Serves 4.

Make It Modern: Substitute fresh salmon, baked for 20 minutes at 400°F, for canned salmon.

Seafood-Noodle Hot Dish

INGREDIENTS

- 2 tablespoons margarine
- 2 pounds flounder or other fish fillets, cut into 1-inch pieces
- 4 cups penne pasta, cooked and drained
- 1 (4-ounce) can sliced mushrooms, drained
- ¼ cup chopped pimientos
- 1 (2.8-ounce) can French fried onions, divided
- 2 (10¾-ounce) cans condensed Cheddar cheese soup, undiluted
- 1 cup whole milk
- 1 teaspoon salt
- 1 teaspoon paprika
- 1 teaspoon Worcestershire sauce

Preheat oven to 350°F.

Melt margarine in a saucepan over medium heat. Add fish; cook on both sides until firm, and place in a large bowl. Combine pasta, mushrooms, pimientos, and ½ onions with fish in bowl. Combine soup, milk, salt, paprika, and Worcestershire sauce in saucepan over medium heat; stir until smooth. Pour soup mixture into fish mixture in bowl; stir carefully. Spoon mixture into a lightly greased, shallow 11x7x2-inch baking dish. Bake 25 minutes or until hot and bubbly around the edges. Top with remaining ½ onions; bake 5 minutes. Serves 6.

Note: Serve with a garden salad and warm bread.

Seafood-Stuffed Manicotti

INGREDIENTS

- 2 tablespoons butter
- 1 medium-size onion, chopped
- ¼ cup finely chopped parsley
- 1 stalk celery, finely chopped
- 1 (14.5-ounce) can tomatoes, cut up and undrained
- 1 cup chicken broth
- ½ teaspoon dried basil
- Pinch white pepper
- ¾ pound cooked fresh crabmeat
- ½ pound cooked and quartered fresh medium-size shrimp (peeled and deveined)
- 3 green onions (including tops), thinly sliced
- 1 cup shredded Fontina cheese
- 8 large manicotti shells, uncooked
- 1 (10-ounce) container refrigerated reduced-fat Alfredo sauce
- ¼ cup grated Parmesan cheese

Preheat oven to 375°F.

Melt butter in a saucepan over medium heat. Add onion; cook while stirring until tender. Stir in parsley, celery, tomatoes, broth, basil, and white pepper. Reduce heat, and simmer 30 minutes. Meanwhile, combine crabmeat, shrimp, green onion, and Fontina cheese in a large bowl. Cook manicotti in salted water until almost tender but still firm; rinse with cold water, and drain well. Spread enough tomato mixture to cover bottom of a lightly greased 13x9x2-inch glass baking dish. Stuff manicotti with seafood mixture; place side by side over tomato mixture in baking dish, adding remaining tomato mixture on sides of manicotti but not on top. Pour Alfredo sauce down center of manicotti. Top with Parmesan cheese. Bake, uncovered, 25 minutes. Serves 4.

Note: A mixed greens salad complements this special seafood-and-pasta hot dish.

Shrimp and Ham Hot Dish

INGREDIENTS

- 2 strips bacon, diced
- ½ cup chopped onion
- ½ cup chopped green bell pepper
- 1 clove garlic, chopped
- 1 (14.5-ounce) can tomatoes, cut up and undrained
- ½ teaspoon salt
- 1 cup cooked fresh shrimp, peeled and deveined
- ½ pound cubed cooked ham
- 1½ cups elbow macaroni, cooked 6 minutes in salted water and drained
- ½ cup dry breadcrumbs, mixed with 2 tablespoons grated Parmesan cheese and 2 tablespoons melted butter

Preheat oven to 350°F.

Cook bacon in a saucepan over medium heat until crisp; drain, reserving ½ drippings in pan, and remove bacon to a large bowl. Cook onion, bell pepper, and garlic in drippings in pan until tender. Add tomatoes and salt to pan; stir until well heated. Add shrimp, ham, and macaroni to bacon in bowl; mix well. Combine tomato mixture with shrimp mixture in bowl. Spoon mixture into a lightly greased 1½-quart glass baking dish. Top with breadcrumb mixture. Bake, uncovered, 30 minutes, until very hot. Serves 4.

Note: This hot dish has a Creole flavor. Serve it with a crisp green salad and crusty rolls.

Tuna Lasagna

INGREDIENTS

- 8 ounces lasagna noodles
- 2 (10½-ounce) cans condensed cream of mushroom soup, undiluted
- ⅔ cup milk
- 1 (16-ounce) bag frozen mixed vegetables, thawed
- 3 (5-ounce) cans tuna, drained
- 16 ounces mild Cheddar cheese, shredded and divided

Preheat oven to 350°F.

Cook lasagna noodles according to package directions; drain. Combine soup and milk in a saucepan over medium heat; bring to a boil. Stir in vegetables until heated. Stir in tuna. Layer ½ noodles, ½ soup mixture, and ½ cheese in a lightly greased 9x13-inch pan. Repeat layers. Bake 30 minutes. Let stand 10–15 minutes before serving. Serves 6.

Tuna-Mushroom Hot Dish

INGREDIENTS

- 1 (12-ounce) package wide egg noodles, cooked and drained
- 3 (5-ounce) cans tuna, drained
- 1 (4-ounce) can mushroom stems and pieces, drained
- 1 tablespoon grated onion
- 1 (10½-ounce) can condensed cream of mushroom soup, undiluted
- 1¼ cups whole milk
- ½ teaspoon salt
- ¼ teaspoon black pepper
- ½ cup crushed saltine crackers, mixed with 3 tablespoons melted butter
- Paprika (optional)

Preheat oven to 350°F.

Combine noodles, tuna, mushrooms, and onion in a large bowl. Combine soup, milk, salt, and pepper in a saucepan over medium heat; stir until just heated. Pour soup mixture over noodle mixture in bowl; mix well. Pour mixture into a lightly greased 11½x7½x2-inch glass baking dish. Top with cracker crumb mixture. Bake, uncovered, 35–45 minutes or until thoroughly heated. Serves 6.

Note: Here's a simple but tasty hot dish. Serve with sliced fresh tomatoes and cucumbers, along with hard rolls.

Tuna Noodle Hot Dish

INGREDIENTS

- 1 (10½-ounce) can condensed cream of mushroom soup, undiluted
- 1¼ cups whole milk
- 6 tablespoons grated Parmesan or Romano cheese
- ¼ cup chopped pimiento-stuffed olives
- 1 tablespoon minced yellow onion
- ¼ teaspoon garlic powder
- 2 (5-ounce) cans tuna, drained and flaked
- Salt to taste
- Ground black pepper to taste
- 3¾ cups (6 ounces) wide egg noodles, cooked according to package directions and drained

Preheat oven to 350°F.

Combine soup and next 8 ingredients in a large bowl; mix well. Stir in noodles. Spoon mixture into a lightly buttered 2-quart baking dish. Bake, uncovered, 30 minutes or until hot, bubbly, and lightly browned. Serves 4.

Note: Tuna and noodles make a popular hot dish combination. Serve with a lettuce-and-tomato salad, tossed with Italian dressing.

Tuna Rotini Hot Dish

INGREDIENTS

- 2 cloves garlic, minced
- 2 eggs, lightly beaten
- ¼ teaspoon salt
- ½ cup Alfredo sauce, homemade or purchased
- 4 cups rotini pasta, cooked according to package directions
- 2 (5-ounce) cans light chunk tuna, drained
- 1½ cups fresh chopped, blanched broccoli or 1 (10-ounce) package frozen chopped broccoli, thawed
- 1 cup seasoned croutons
- 2 tablespoons Parmesan cheese

Preheat oven to 350°F.

Mix together garlic, eggs, salt, and Alfredo sauce in a large bowl until blended. Stir in pasta, tuna, and broccoli. Pour mixture into a lightly greased, shallow 2-quart glass baking dish. Bake, covered, 25 minutes or until mixture is set. Remove from oven; top with croutons and cheese. Serves 6.

Note: Serve this hot dish with a molded strawberry-fruit gelatin salad and hard rolls.

Fish 'n' Potato Hot Dish

INGREDIENTS

- 4 medium-size potatoes, peeled, boiled until almost tender, drained, and cut into ⅛-inch-thick slices
- 1 teaspoon all-purpose flour
- 1 small onion, sliced into rings
- ¼ teaspoon ground black pepper
- ¾ cup milk, divided
- 1½ pounds cod fillets
- 1 tablespoon grated Parmesan cheese
- 2 tablespoons minced fresh parsley
- ¼ teaspoon paprika

Preheat oven to 375°F.

Place potatoes into a lightly greased, shallow 2-quart baking dish. Sprinkle with flour. Top with onion rings. Sprinkle with black pepper. Pour ½ cup milk over potatoes. Place fish on top; pour remaining ¼ cup milk over fish. Sprinkle with Parmesan cheese. Cover and bake 25 minutes or until fish flakes easily with a fork. Remove from oven; sprinkle with parsley and paprika. Serves 4.

Note: Minnesotans love cod and serve it many ways. Some folks have a traditional Christmas dish called lutefisk, which is served with drawn butter if you are Norwegian or a cream sauce if you are Swedish. This hot dish is another way of serving codfish.

Fish Sticks Au Gratin

INGREDIENTS

3 medium-size potatoes, very thinly sliced and divided

2 tablespoons all-purpose flour, divided

4 tablespoons butter, divided

Salt and black pepper to taste

1½ cups grated Cheddar cheese, divided

1 cup whole milk, heated and divided

1 (10-ounce) package frozen battered or breaded fish sticks or fillets

Preheat oven to 450°F.

Layer ½ potato slices, 1 tablespoon flour, 2 tablespoons butter, salt, pepper, ½ cup cheese, and ½ cup hot milk in a lightly greased 2-quart glass baking dish. Repeat layers. Place fish on top. Top with remaining ½ cup cheese. Bake, covered, 20 minutes. Uncover; bake 20 minutes. Serves 4.

Note: This is a hot dish that most kids will like. Serve with peas and carrots, along with warm rolls.

Cheesy Fish, Rice, and Asparagus

INGREDIENTS

- 2 cups cooked long-grain white rice
- 1 pound fresh, tender asparagus spears, cut into 1-inch pieces, blanched 1 minute, and drained
- 2 pounds orange roughy fillets, cut into serving portions
- 3 tablespoons butter
- 1 medium-size onion, chopped
- 1 clove garlic, minced
- 5 tablespoons all-purpose flour
- 1 cup whole milk
- ¼ teaspoon salt
- ¼ teaspoon white pepper
- 1 cup shredded Cheddar cheese
- ¾ cup unseasoned dry bread-crumbs, mixed with 5 tablespoons grated Parmesan cheese

Preheat oven to 350°F.

Spoon rice evenly onto bottom of a lightly greased 13x9x2-inch glass baking dish. Top evenly with asparagus. Place fish fillets over asparagus. Melt butter in a saucepan over medium heat; add onion, and cook while stirring 2 minutes (do not brown). Add garlic; cook while stirring a few seconds. Gradually stir in flour until blended. Gradually add milk, stirring constantly, until slightly thickened. Stir in salt, pepper, and Cheddar cheese until melted; pour milk mixture over top of fish in baking dish. Top with breadcrumb mixture. Cover; bake 35 minutes. Uncover; bake 10 minutes. Serves 4.

Note: Serve a crisp salad and rolls to complete this meal.

Herbed Rice 'n' Fish Hot Dish

INGREDIENTS

- 1 teaspoon chicken bouillon granules, mixed in 1½ cups boiling water
- ½ cup long-grain white rice, uncooked
- ¼ teaspoon Italian seasoning
- ¼ teaspoon garlic powder
- 1 (10-ounce) package frozen chopped broccoli, thawed and drained
- 1 (2.8-ounce) can French fried onions, divided
- 1 tablespoon grated Parmesan cheese
- 1 pound unbreaded fish fillets, fresh or frozen (thawed)
- ½ cup shredded Cheddar cheese

Preheat oven to 400°F.

Combine hot bouillon, rice, Italian seasoning, and garlic powder in a lightly greased 11x7x2-inch baking dish. Bake, covered, 10 minutes. Top with broccoli, ½ onions, and Parmesan cheese. Place fish diagonally down center of dish. Bake, covered, 25 minutes or until fish flakes easily with a fork. Gently stir rice. Top fish with shredded Cheddar cheese and remaining ½ onions. Bake, uncovered, 3 minutes or until onions are golden brown. Serves 4.

Note: Serve with a tossed salad and hard rolls.

Oyster Wild Rice

INGREDIENTS

- 2 **cups soft breadcrumbs, mixed with ½ cup melted butter and divided**
- ½ **cup long-grain wild rice, cooked according to package directions and divided**
- 1 **cup raw oysters, liquor reserved**
- 2 **tablespoons butter, cut up**

Chicken broth

Preheat oven to 350˚F.

Layer 1 cup breadcrumb mixture, ½ rice, and oysters in a buttered 1½-quart glass baking dish. Dot with butter, and top with remaining ½ rice. Add enough chicken broth to reserved oyster liquor to measure 1½ cups; pour over rice. Top with remaining 1 cup breadcrumb mixture. Cover with aluminum foil. Bake 30 minutes. Remove foil, and bake 15 minutes or until crumbs are golden. Serves 4.

Note: Here's a simple hot dish to make for special friends.

Nelan's Seafood Hot Dish

INGREDIENTS

- 5 tablespoons butter
- 1 large onion, chopped
- 1 tablespoon chopped garlic
- ½ cup chopped green bell pepper
- ¼ cup chopped fresh parsley
- ¾ cup long-grain white rice, uncooked
- 1 (10½-ounce) can condensed cream of mushroom soup, mixed with ¾ cup milk
- 2 cups fresh peeled, deveined shrimp
- 1½ cups fresh crabmeat, picked over
- ½ teaspoon salt
- ¼ teaspoon ground black pepper
- ½ cup unseasoned dry bread-crumbs, mixed with 1 tablespoon melted butter

Preheat oven to 350°F.

Melt butter in a saucepan over medium heat. Stir in onion, garlic, bell pepper, and parsley; cook while stirring until vegetables are soft but not brown. Add rice and soup; stir until thoroughly heated. Add shrimp, crabmeat, salt, and pepper; stir to combine. Pour mixture into a lightly greased 2½-quart glass baking dish. Cover and bake 10 minutes. Top with breadcrumb mixture; bake 35 minutes or until rice is tender. Serves 6.

Note: Salad and crusty bread complete this tasty meal.

Salmon-Rice Hot Dish

INGREDIENTS

- 1 cup long-grain white rice, cooked in salted water 15 minutes and drained
- 1 tablespoon fresh lemon juice
- ¼ cup chopped fresh parsley
- 4 tablespoons butter, divided
- 1 pound salmon fillet, cut into 2-inch pieces
- 1½ pounds fresh asparagus, cut in half crosswise and blanched
- ½ cup finely chopped onion
- 3 tablespoons all-purpose flour
- 1½ cups chicken stock or broth
- ½ cup heavy cream
- ¼ teaspoon salt
- Pinch ground black pepper
- ½ cup Parmesan cheese, divided

Preheat oven to 450°F.

Combine rice, lemon juice, parsley, and 1 tablespoon butter in a bowl. Spoon rice mixture into a lightly greased, shallow 2-quart glass baking dish. Place salmon on top of rice. Place asparagus on top of salmon. Cook onion in remaining 3 tablespoons butter in a saucepan over medium heat until tender. Gradually stir in flour until well blended. Add stock; stir until thickened. Stir in cream, salt, pepper, and 4 tablespoons cheese. Pour cream mixture over asparagus. Sprinkle with remaining 4 tablespoons cheese. Bake 25 minutes or until very hot and browned on top. Serves 4.

Note: This is a pretty hot dish. Garnish with sliced fresh tomatoes before serving.

Salmon with Saffron Rice

INGREDIENTS

- 1 cup chopped onion
- 2 tablespoons olive oil
- 4 cloves garlic, chopped
- ¼ teaspoon dried thyme, crushed
- 5 cups cooked (in salted water) long-grain white rice
- 1 teaspoon saffron threads, crushed and soaked in 5 tablespoons boiling water
- 2 tablespoons butter
- 1 pound skinless salmon fillet, cut into 4 portions and lightly seasoned with salt and ground black pepper

Garnish: parsley sprigs

Preheat oven to 350°F.

Cook onion in olive oil in a saucepan over medium heat until golden, about 5 minutes. Add garlic; cook while stirring a few seconds. Place onion mixture in a bowl. Stir in thyme. Stir in rice and saffron mixture. Melt butter in saucepan over medium heat. Fry salmon in butter 2 minutes on each side. Spoon ½ rice mixture into a lightly greased 2-quart glass baking dish. Place salmon over rice. Spoon remaining ½ rice mixture over salmon. Cover and bake 40 minutes. Garnish, if desired. Serves 4.

Note: Serve with a lettuce-and-tomato salad tossed with Italian dressing, along with buttered peas.

Scallops 'n' Shrimp Hot Dish

INGREDIENTS

- ¾ cup small fresh scallops, liquid reserved
- 2 eggs, lightly beaten
- 2 cups cooked long-grain white rice
- ¾ cup cut up boiled fresh shrimp (peeled and deveined)
- 2 tablespoons diced onion
- 2 tablespoons butter
- ¼ cup ketchup
- ½ teaspoon celery salt
- ¾ teaspoon curry powder

Preheat oven to 350°F.

Combine liquid from scallops with eggs in a large bowl; stir in scallops, rice, and shrimp. Cook onion in butter in a small sauce-pan until lightly browned. Add ketchup, celery salt, and curry powder to onion in pan; stir onion mixture into rice mixture in bowl. Spoon mixture into a lightly greased, shallow 1½-quart baking dish. Bake 30 minutes or until firm. Serves 6.

Note: Serve with a crisp green salad and French bread.

Shrimp and Rice Hot Dish

INGREDIENTS

4 cups chicken broth

Pinch crushed saffron

3 tablespoons olive oil

1 medium-size onion,
 finely chopped

2 tablespoons finely chopped
 green bell pepper

2 cloves garlic, finely chopped

2 cups long-grain white rice,
 uncooked

Salt and black pepper to taste

2 cups peeled and deveined raw
 shrimp, cut into ½-inch pieces

½ cup diced cooked
 smoked sausage

Preheat oven to 400°F.

Heat broth in a saucepan over medium heat; stir in saffron, and reduce heat to low. Heat oil in a large saucepan over medium-high heat. Add onion and bell pepper; cook while stirring 5 minutes. Add garlic; cook while stirring a few seconds. Add rice; cook while stirring 1 minute. Add salt and pepper. Stir in broth mixture. Add shrimp and sausage; stir to mix well. Pour mixture into a lightly greased, shallow 2-quart glass baking dish. Bake 40 minutes or until rice is done. Serves 4.

Note: This is almost paella! Serve it with a crisp green salad.

Tuna-Rice Hot Dish

INGREDIENTS

- 1 tablespoon butter
- ½ cup chopped onion
- 2 cups cooked long-grain white rice
- 2 (5-ounce) cans tuna in oil, drained and flaked
- 1½ cups milk
- 3 eggs, lightly beaten
- ¼ teaspoon salt
- Pinch black pepper

Preheat oven to 350°F.

Melt butter in a saucepan over medium heat. Add onion; cook while stirring until tender. Combine onion mixture, rice, and next 5 ingredients in a large bowl. Spoon mixture into a buttered 2½-quart glass baking dish. Place baking dish in a baking pan filled with 1 inch of water. Bake 45 minutes. Serves 6.

Note: This hot dish recipe dates back to the early 1950s. Serve it with a lettuce-and-tomato salad and rolls.

Almond Crab Hot Dish

INGREDIENTS

- 1 (10½-ounce) can condensed cream of mushroom soup, undiluted
- 1 cup chopped celery
- ¼ cup chopped onion
- 1½ cups chow mein noodles
- 1 (8-ounce) can sliced water chestnuts, drained
- 1 (4-ounce) can mushroom pieces, undrained
- 1 teaspoon Worcestershire sauce
- 1 (6-ounce) package frozen crabmeat, thawed and liquid reserved
- 6 tablespoons toasted slivered almonds

Preheat oven to 350°F.

Stir together soup, celery, onion, noodles, water chestnuts, mushrooms, and Worcestershire sauce in a large bowl. Fold in crabmeat and reserved liquid. Spoon mixture into a lightly greased 1½-quart baking dish. Top evenly with almonds. Bake 30 minutes or until hot and bubbly. Serves 4.

Note: Serve with a crisp green salad and rolls.

 Make It Modern: Substitute fresh crabmeat for frozen crabmeat.

Chopstick Tuna Hot Dish

INGREDIENTS

- ½ (10½-ounce) can condensed cream of mushroom soup, undiluted
- ½ cup skim milk
- ¼ cup water
- 2 (5-ounce) cans tuna, drained
- 1 (10-ounce) package frozen peas
- 1 (8-ounce) can sliced water chestnuts, undrained
- 1 medium-size tomato, peeled and diced
- ½ cup chopped celery
- 5 tablespoons sliced green onions
- 2 tablespoons light soy sauce
- 1½ cups chow mein noodles, divided

Preheat oven to 375°F.

Combine soup, milk, and water in a large bowl; stir to blend. Add tuna; mix well. Add peas, next 5 ingredients, and ½ noodles. Mix lightly. Spoon mixture into a lightly greased 1½-quart glass baking dish. Top with remaining ½ noodles. Bake 25–30 minutes until very hot. Serves 6.

Note: When you're looking for yet another way to prepare tuna, try this Asian-style hot dish.

 Make It Modern: Substitute fresh tuna, cooked, in place of canned tuna.

Friday's Fish and Shrimp

INGREDIENTS

1 cup chopped onion

1 tablespoon olive oil

3 cloves garlic, finely chopped

1 (28-ounce) can stewed tomatoes, undrained

½ cup water

Salt and ground black pepper to taste

3 tablespoons chopped fresh parsley

¼ teaspoon dried oregano, crushed

1 pound cod or haddock, boned

½ pound fresh shrimp, peeled and deveined

6 ounces feta cheese, cut into chunks

Hot cooked rice or orzo pasta

Preheat oven to 400°F.

Cook onion in oil in a saucepan over medium heat until tender. Add garlic; cook while stirring a few seconds. Add tomatoes, ½ cup water, salt, pepper, parsley, and oregano. Bring to a boil; reduce heat, cover, and simmer 15 minutes, stirring often. Spoon tomato mixture into a lightly greased 2½-quart glass baking dish. Arrange fish on top. Cover and bake 15 minutes. Add shrimp and feta cheese. Cover and bake 15 minutes. Serve over hot cooked rice or orzo pasta. Serves 6.

Note: A tossed salad goes well with this dish.

Hearty Shrimp Hot Dish

INGREDIENTS

- 1 tablespoon olive oil
- 1 cup chopped onion
- 3 cloves garlic, thinly sliced
- 1 medium-size green bell pepper, chopped
- 2 (15.5-ounce) cans cannellini beans, rinsed and drained
- 1 (14.5-ounce) can tomatoes, diced
- 1 cup low-sodium chicken broth
- ½ teaspoon salt
- Pinch ground black pepper
- ¼ teaspoon dried basil
- ¼ teaspoon dried thyme
- ½ cup kalamata olives, pitted and halved
- 1 pound fresh shrimp, peeled and deveined
- ½ cup dry breadcrumbs, mixed with ¼ cup Parmesan cheese

Preheat oven to 400°F.

Heat oil in a large saucepan over medium heat; cook onion, garlic, and bell pepper while stirring until tender, about 4 minutes. Add beans, tomatoes, broth, salt, pepper, basil, thyme, and olives. Bring to a slow boil. Reduce heat. Add shrimp, and simmer 4 minutes. Spoon mixture into a lightly greased 3-quart baking dish. Top with breadcrumb mixture. Bake, uncovered, 25 minutes or until bubbly and very hot. Serves 8.

Note: This shrimp hot dish is much like a cassoulet.

Tuna Casserole

INGREDIENTS

- **2 tablespoons butter**
- **2 tablespoons all-purpose flour**
- **½ teaspoon onion salt**
- **1 (10½-ounce) can cream of celery or cream of mushroom soup, undiluted**
- **1⅓ cups milk**
- **½ cup shredded Cheddar cheese**
- **2 (5-ounce) cans tuna, drained**
- **1 cup green peas**
- **1 package refrigerated buttermilk biscuits**

Preheat oven to 350°F.

Melt butter in a saucepan over medium heat; stir in flour and onion salt. Stir in soup and milk. Cook until thick and bubbly. Stir in cheese, tuna, and peas. Pour mixture into a lightly greased 9-inch baking dish. Cut each biscuit into 4 pieces. Arrange on top of tuna mixture. Bake 20–25 minutes or until biscuits are golden. Serves 6.

 Make It Modern: Substitute your favorite homemade buttermilk biscuit recipe for canned biscuits.

Breakfast & Eggs

Helen's Ham and Eggs

INGREDIENTS

- 12 slices white bread
- 1 pound diced cooked ham
- 2 cups shredded Cheddar cheese
- 6 large eggs
- 3 cups whole milk
- 2 teaspoons Worcestershire sauce
- ¾ teaspoon dry mustard
- ½ teaspoon salt
- ¼ teaspoon ground black pepper
- Pinch ground cayenne pepper
- 1 small yellow onion, finely chopped
- 3 tablespoons chopped green bell pepper
- 1 tablespoon chopped red bell pepper
- ¼ cup butter, melted
- 1 cup crushed Corn Flakes cereal

Preheat oven to 350°F.

Remove crusts from bread; place 6 slices on bottom of a lightly greased 13x9x2-inch baking dish. Top evenly with ham and cheese. Top with remaining 6 slices bread. Beat eggs lightly in a large bowl; add milk and next 8 ingredients. Pour egg mixture over bread in dish. Cover and refrigerate 8 hours. Remove cover; spoon butter evenly over top. Top with Corn Flakes. Bake, uncovered, 1 hour or until a knife inserted in center comes out clean. Let stand a few minutes before serving. Serves 8.

Note: Serve this tasty hot dish for brunch or supper with fresh fruit and cinnamon-apple muffins.

Overnight Ham 'n' Eggs

INGREDIENTS

- 6 slices bread
- 2 tablespoons butter, softened
- 2 cups shredded Cheddar cheese
- ¾ pound thinly sliced cooked ham
- 1 (8-ounce) package fresh mushrooms, sliced and sautéed in 1 tablespoon butter
- 2 (4-ounce) cans diced green chilies
- 2 cups shredded Monterey Jack cheese
- 6 eggs
- 2 cups whole milk
- 1½ teaspoons salt
- ½ teaspoon paprika
- ½ teaspoon dry mustard
- ¼ teaspoon ground black pepper
- ¼ teaspoon onion salt
- ¼ teaspoon dried basil

Preheat oven to 350°F.

Spread bread with butter on one side only; place, buttered-side down, in a lightly greased 13x9x2-inch glass baking dish. Top with Cheddar cheese. Layer ham, mushrooms, and chilies on top of cheese in baking dish. Top with Monterey Jack cheese. Beat eggs in a medium-size bowl. Add milk and next 6 ingredients to bowl; stir until blended. Pour egg mixture over cheese in baking dish. Cover with plastic wrap; refrigerate overnight. Remove from refrigerator 1 hour before baking. Remove plastic wrap. Bake, uncovered, 50 minutes. Let stand 10 minutes before serving. Serves 6.

Note: This hearty egg hot dish is perfect for a late family breakfast with toast and fresh fruit juice.

Spuds-Ham-Eggs Hot Dish

INGREDIENTS

- 1 (2-pound) bag frozen hash brown potatoes
- 2 cups diced cooked ham
- 2 cups shredded Swiss cheese
- 1½ tablespoons butter
- 1 large red bell pepper, cut into ½-inch strips
- 1 (8-ounce) package fresh mushrooms, sliced
- 6 large eggs, lightly beaten
- ½ cup whole milk
- 1 cup cottage cheese
- ¼ teaspoon ground black pepper

Preheat oven to 350˚F.

Layer ½ potatoes into a lightly greased 13x9x2-inch glass baking dish. Top with ham and cheese. Melt butter in a saucepan over medium heat. Add bell pepper and mushrooms; cook while stirring 5 minutes or until tender. Spoon mushroom mixture over cheese in baking dish; top with remaining ½ potatoes. Combine eggs, milk, cottage cheese, and black pepper in a bowl; beat until well blended. Pour egg mixture over potatoes in baking dish. Bake, uncovered, 50 minutes or until light brown and center is set. Serves 8.

Note: This is a good hot dish for brunch or a light supper. Serve it with warm muffins, quick breads, and fresh fruit.

Tangy Ham 'n' Eggs

INGREDIENTS

- 2 (1-pound) loaves Italian-style bread, cut into 1-inch cubes
- 6 cups cubed cooked ham
- 1½ pounds Monterey Jack cheese, cubed
- 1 medium-size onion, chopped
- ¼ cup butter
- 16 eggs, lightly beaten
- 7 cups whole milk
- ½ cup prepared mustard
- ½ teaspoon Worcestershire sauce
- Garnish: chopped fresh parsley

Preheat oven to 350°F.

Mix together bread, ham, and cheese in a large bowl; place equal amounts bread mixture into bottom of 2 lightly greased 13x9x2-inch glass baking dishes. Cook onion in butter in a saucepan over medium heat until just tender. Remove onion mixture to a large bowl; add eggs and next 3 ingredients, and mix well. Pour equal amounts egg mixture over bread mixture in each baking dish. Cover and refrigerate 8 hours. Remove from refrigerator 30 minutes before baking. Bake, uncovered, 55–65 minutes or until a knife inserted in center comes out clean. Garnish with parsley, if desired. Serves 24.

Note: This egg hot dish is perfect for brunch. Serve it with fresh fruit, juices, and assorted warm muffins.

The Girls Ham 'n' Eggs

INGREDIENTS

- 3 cups frozen shredded hash brown potatoes
- ¾ cup shredded Monterey Jack cheese
- 1 cup diced cooked ham
- ¼ cup chopped green onion (including tops)
- 4 eggs
- 1 (12-ounce) can evaporated milk
- ¼ teaspoon ground black pepper
- Pinch salt

Preheat oven to 350°F.

Place potatoes in bottom of a lightly greased 8-inch square glass baking dish. Top with cheese, ham, and onion. Beat together eggs, milk, pepper, and salt in a bowl. Pour egg mixture over onion in baking dish. Cover and refrigerate 3 hours. Remove from refrigerator 30 minutes before baking. Bake, uncovered, 55–60 minutes or until a knife inserted in center comes out clean. Serves 6.

Note: This is the egg hot dish the girls will purr for. You can refrigerate it overnight and bake it the next day. Serve with slices of toast and strawberry jam.

Bacon, Cheddar, and Potato Pie

INGREDIENTS

1 **pound small potatoes, cooked and sliced**

½ **cup shredded Cheddar cheese**

⅓ **cup cooked and crumbled bacon**

2 **green onions, sliced**

6 **eggs**

¼ **cup milk**

⅓ **cup Miracle Whip**

Preheat oven to 350°F.

Layer potatoes in a lightly greased 9-inch baking pan. Top with cheese, bacon, and onion. Mix together eggs and milk in a bowl until well blended; stir in Miracle Whip. Pour egg mixture over potato mixture in pan. Bake 25–30 minutes or until center is set. Let stand 10 minutes. Serves 6.

Hash Brown Bake

INGREDIENTS

- 1 (2-pound) bag hash browns
- 1 (12-ounce) carton sour cream
- 1 (10½-ounce) can condensed cream of potato soup, undiluted
- 1 (10½-ounce) can condensed cream of celery soup, undiluted
- 1 (10¾-ounce) can Cheddar cheese soup
- Salt and pepper
- Parsley flakes
- ½ cup grated Cheddar cheese

Preheat oven to 350°F.

Stir together hash browns, sour cream, soups, salt, and pepper. Spoon into a lightly greased 9x13-inch baking dish. Top with parsley flakes and cheese. Bake 1¼ hours. Serves 6.

Make It Modern: Garnish with 3–4 strips cooked and crumbled bacon before serving.

Morning Mix-up

INGREDIENTS

2 cups frozen hash browns

1 cup chopped cooked ham

½ cup chopped onion

2 tablespoons vegetable oil

6 eggs

Salt and pepper

1 cup shredded Cheddar cheese

Sauté hash browns, ham, and onion in vegetable oil in large skillet over medium heat 10 minutes. Beat eggs, salt, and pepper in a small bowl. Add to skillet; cook, stirring occasionally, until eggs are set. Remove from heat, and gently stir in cheese. Serves 6.

Egg and Sausage Hot Dish

INGREDIENTS

- 8 ounces sweet or hot Italian sausage, casings removed, crumbled
- 2 teaspoons olive oil
- 2 cups red bell pepper strips
- 2 medium-size onions, thinly sliced
- 1 teaspoon salt, divided
- 4 large eggs
- 5 cups whole milk
- Pinch ground black pepper
- 1 (1-pound) loaf Italian bread, sliced ½-inch thick and quartered
- 1 cup shredded Fontina cheese

Preheat oven to 350°F.

Cook sausage in a saucepan over medium heat until browned; drain, and remove sausage to a small bowl. Heat oil in saucepan. Add bell pepper, onion, and ¼ teaspoon salt. Cook while stirring 15 minutes. Beat eggs, milk, remaining ¾ teaspoon salt, and black pepper in a large bowl. Place enough bread to cover bottom of a lightly greased 13x9x2-inch glass baking dish. Spread ½ onion mixture over bread; top with ½ sausage, and then sprinkle with ½ cheese. Pour ½ egg mixture over all. Repeat layers. Cover with plastic wrap; refrigerate overnight. Remove from refrigerator 1 hour before baking. Discard plastic wrap. Cover with aluminum foil; bake 30 minutes. Uncover; bake 25 minutes. Serves 8.

Note: Here's a good egg dish to fix ahead of time for a brunch.

Sausage 'n' Eggs Hot Dish

INGREDIENTS

- 1 (1-pound) package breakfast sausage
- 1 (8-ounce) can refrigerated crescent roll dough
- 2 cups shredded mozzarella cheese
- 4 eggs
- ¾ cup whole milk
- ¾ teaspoon salt
- Pinch ground black pepper

Preheat oven to 425˚F.

Crumble sausage into a saucepan, and cook while stirring over medium heat until sausage is no longer pink; drain. Line bottom of a buttered 13x9x2-inch glass baking dish with crescent roll dough, firmly pressing perforations together to seal. Sprinkle with sausage and cheese. Combine eggs and next 3 ingredients in a bowl; beat well, and pour over cheese in baking dish. Bake 15 minutes or until eggs are set. Let stand 5 minutes. Cut into serving-size squares; serve immediately. Serves 6.

Note: This is an easy hot dish to make for a quick yet special breakfast or brunch.

Breakfast Burritos Hot Dish

INGREDIENTS

- 8 strips bacon
- 8 large fresh mushrooms, sliced
- 6 green onions, sliced
- 6 tablespoons chopped green bell pepper
- 2 cloves garlic, chopped
- 8 large eggs
- ¼ cup sour cream
- 1 cup shredded Cheddar cheese, divided
- 3 tablespoons taco sauce
- 1 tablespoon butter
- 4 (9-inch) flour tortillas

Preheat oven to 350°F.

Cook bacon in a saucepan over medium heat until crisp; drain, reserving 1 tablespoon drippings in pan. Crumble bacon into a large bowl. Add mushrooms, onion, bell pepper, and garlic to drippings in saucepan. Cook while stirring until tender; remove mushroom mixture, and add to bacon in bowl. Beat eggs and sour cream in a large bowl until blended. Stir in ¼ cup cheese and taco sauce. Melt butter in saucepan; add egg mixture. Cook, stirring constantly, until eggs are set. Stir bacon mixture into egg mixture. Spoon mixture down center of tortillas; roll up. Place, seam-side down, in a lightly greased 11x7x2-inch baking dish. Top with remaining ¾ cup cheese. Bake 5 minutes or until cheese melts. Serves 4.

Note: Top this dish with more sour cream when serving.

Chilaquile Hot Dish

INGREDIENTS

- 1 tablespoon corn oil
- 1 cup chopped onion
- 1 teaspoon minced garlic
- 12 corn tortillas, torn into 1-inch pieces
- 2 cups shredded Monterey Jack cheese, divided
- 2 (4-ounce) cans chopped mild green chilies
- 4 large eggs
- 2 cups buttermilk
- ½ teaspoon salt
- ¼ teaspoon ground black pepper
- ⅛ teaspoon cumin
- ⅛ teaspoon dried oregano

Preheat oven to 350°F.

Heat oil in a saucepan over medium-low heat. Add onion and garlic; cook while stirring 5 minutes. Spread ½ tortillas onto bottom of a lightly greased 11½x7½x2-inch glass baking dish. Sprinkle ½ cheese and 1 can chilies over top. Sprinkle ½ onion mixture over chilies. Layer remaining ½ tortillas, ½ cheese, 1 can chilies, and ½ onion mixture. Whisk together eggs and next 5 ingredients. Pour over all. Bake 45 minutes or until eggs are set and browned on top. Serves 6.

Note: This dish is a good way to use leftover tortillas. Serve for lunch or a light supper. A crisp green salad completes the meal.

Sam's Burritos

INGREDIENTS

- 1 large green bell pepper, chopped
- ¾ cup chopped onion
- 2 tablespoons butter
- 8 eggs, lightly beaten with a pinch of salt and ground black pepper
- ½ cup shredded Cheddar cheese
- ½ cup shredded Monterey Jack cheese
- 1½ cups picante sauce
- 8 (8-inch) flour tortillas
- Sour cream

Preheat oven to 350˚F.

Cook bell pepper and onion in butter in a large saucepan over medium heat until tender but not brown. Combine eggs and cheeses in a bowl. Add egg mixture to onion mixture in pan; cook while stirring until eggs are set and cheese is melted. Remove from heat. Heat picante sauce in a medium saucepan over medium heat; dip each tortilla into sauce, one at a time. Spoon ½ cup egg mixture down center of each tortilla. Fold 2 sides over egg mixture; fold ends under, and place into a lightly greased 13x9x2-inch glass baking dish. Top with remaining picante sauce. Bake 10 minutes or until very hot. Top with sour cream just before serving. Serves 8.

Note: When Sam first tasted a flour tortilla, it reminded him of lefse (a traditional Norwegian flatbread)—a bit thicker, but something he could get used to. Serve this burrito hot dish for brunch along with assorted fresh fruit.

Breakfast Pizza

INGREDIENTS

- 1 (8-ounce) package refrigerated crescent rolls
- 1 (8–12 ounce) package brown-and-serve sausage, cooked and drained
- 2 cups shredded Cheddar cheese
- 4 lightly beaten eggs
- ¾ cup milk
- ¼ teaspoon ground black pepper
- ¼ teaspoon oregano
- 2 tablespoons chopped onion
- 1 cup mozzarella cheese

Preheat oven to 350°F.

Spread crescent roll dough into a lightly greased 9x13-inch baking pan. Cut sausage into small pieces, and sprinkle over dough. Top with Cheddar cheese. Combine eggs, milk, pepper, oregano, and onion in a bowl. Pour over Cheddar cheese in pan. Top with mozzarella cheese. Bake 25–35 minutes. Serves 4–6.

Note: You may also add chopped green bell pepper or sliced mushrooms for more toppings.

Cinnamon French Toast

INGREDIENTS

2 cups whole milk

¼ teaspoon vanilla extract

3 eggs, lightly beaten

12 slices whole wheat bread, cut in half crosswise

2 tablespoons butter, melted

½ cup powdered sugar

1½ cups golden raisins

2½ teaspoons ground cinnamon

Preheat oven to 400°F.

Combine milk, vanilla, and eggs in a medium-size bowl; whisk until blended. Dip bread slices in milk mixture to coat. Layer ⅓ coated bread slices on bottom of a buttered 9x9-inch square glass baking dish; drizzle evenly with ⅓ butter, ⅓ sugar, and ½ raisins. Repeat layers once, going a different direction with the bread. Top with remaining ⅓ bread, ⅓ butter, and ⅓ sugar. Top with ground cinnamon. Cover and bake 25 minutes. Remove cover; bake 15 minutes. Serves 6.

Note: Tempt the teenagers with this breakfast dish.

Make It Modern: Substitute 12 slices buttermilk bread for whole wheat bread.

Scrambled Eggs 'n' Broccoli

INGREDIENTS

- 4 tablespoons butter, divided
- ¼ cup all-purpose flour
- 2 cups whole milk
- 2 cups shredded Cheddar cheese
- 1 cup sliced fresh mushrooms
- ¼ cup finely chopped onion
- 12 eggs, lightly beaten
- 1 teaspoon salt
- 1 (10-ounce) package frozen chopped broccoli, cooked and drained
- 1 cup soft breadcrumbs, tossed with 1 tablespoon melted butter

Preheat oven to 350°F.

Melt 2 tablespoons butter in a saucepan over medium heat. Add flour; cook while stirring until flour mixture begins to bubble. Gradually stir in milk. Bring to a boil; cook while stirring 2 minutes. Remove from heat. Stir in cheese until melted. Melt remaining 2 tablespoons butter in a large saucepan over medium heat. Add mushrooms and onion; cook while stirring until tender. Stir eggs and salt into mushroom mixture in pan; cook while stirring until eggs are set. Add cheese mixture and broccoli to egg mixture; mix well. Pour mixture into a lightly greased 11½x7½x2-inch glass baking dish. Top with breadcrumb mixture. Cover and refrigerate overnight. Remove from refrigerator 30 minutes before baking. Bake, uncovered, 30 minutes. Serves 6.

Note: This make-ahead egg dish is perfect for a lazy morning breakfast. Serve with fruit juice along with biscuits or buttered toast.

ALTERNATIVES FOR CANNED SOUPS: MAKE YOUR OWN!

Many hot dish recipes call for canned soups; that's a surefire way to make a quick meal, but if you want to make a fresher or little bit healthier option, consider incorporating your own soup recipe instead. Each of these recipes will replace one can (10–11 ounces) of condensed soup.

Replacement for Cream of Chicken Soup

INGREDIENTS

- ¼ **cup flour**
- ¾ **cup chicken broth**
- ½ **cup milk**
- ⅛ **tsp onion powder**
- ⅛ **tsp garlic powder**
- ¼ **tsp parsley flakes or ½ teaspoon minced fresh parsley (optional)**
- **salt and pepper to taste**

Whisk flour into broth in a medium saucepan until smooth. Add remaining ingredients and whisk to combine. Cook over medium-low heat, while stirring constantly, until thick and bubbly. Reduce heat to low, and continue to cook, while stirring, for an additional 2 minutes.

Replacement for Cream of Celery Soup

INGREDIENTS

- **5 tablespoons flour**
- **½ cup vegetable broth**
- **1 tablespoon butter**
- **¼ cup minced celery**
- **¾ cup milk**
- **salt and pepper to taste**

In a small bowl, whisk flour into broth until smooth; set aside. Melt butter in a medium saucepan over medium-low heat; sauté celery in butter until tender. Add flour mixture, milk, salt, and pepper to saucepan. Heat, while stirring constantly, until thick and bubbly. Reduce heat to low, and continue to cook, while stirring, for an additional 2 minutes

Replacement for Cream of Mushroom Soup

INGREDIENTS

- **5 tablespoons flour**
- **½ cup vegetable broth**
- **1 tablespoon butter**
- **¼ cup minced fresh mushrooms**
- **¾ cup milk**
- **salt and pepper to taste**

In a small bowl, whisk flour into broth until smooth; set aside. Melt butter in a medium saucepan over medium-low heat; sauté mushrooms in butter until soft. Add flour mixture, milk, salt, and pepper to saucepan. Heat, while stirring constantly, until thick and bubbly. Reduce heat to low, and continue to cook, while stirring, for an additional 2 minutes.

INDEX